I DO NOT LIKE THEE, DOCTOR FELL

BERNARD FARRELL

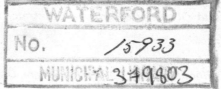

CO·OP
BOOKS

ISBN 0 905441 16 8

First published in 1979 by Co-op Books Publishing Ltd., 50 Merrion Square, Dublin 2, Ireland.
Co-op Books is owned and operated by members of the Irish Writers' Co-operative, which exists to provide outlets for Irish writing through publications and the organisation of public readings.

The Irish Writers' Co-operative acknowledges the assistance of An Chomairle Ealaíon in the publication of this book.
Special thanks to Douglas Kennedy, Administrator, The Peacock Theatre.

Design: Brendan Foreman
Typesetting: Gifford & Craven, 50 Merrion Square, Dublin 2.
Photographs: Courtesy of Fergus Bourke

DEDICATION

"For My Parents."

"I Do Not Like Thee, Dr. Fell" was first presented at the Peacock Theatre, Dublin, on March 15th 1979 with the following cast:

Paddy . . . . John Molloy
Joe . . . . Garrett Keogh
Suzy . . . . Billie Morton
Roger . . . . Liam Neeson
Peter . . . . Tom Hickey
Maureen . . . . Eileen Colgan
Rita . . . . Kathleen Barrington

The play was directed by Paul Brennan and designed by Frank Conway. Lighting by Tony Wakefield.

NOTE

Sound effects — not included here in the stage directions — were used in both the original Peacock Theatre production and in the transfer of the play to Cork. While they are not absolutely essential to the workings of the play, their importance is appreciable.

The effects used in Cork were:
1 Before Act One, Scene One: Confused sounds of a baby and of a train.
2 Before Act One, Scene Two: Sound of a cat and of a train.
3 Before Act Two, Scene One: Sound of a baby gurgling, not crying.
4 End of Act Two, Scene Two: The last two bars of 'The Laughing Policeman' recording between Suzy's last line and Blackout.

B.F.

BIOGRAPHICAL NOTE

Bernard Farrell has scripted for RTE and had short stories and features widely published. In 1974, he joined the Lantern Theatre Workshop. His first one-act play, "Goodbye Smiler, It's Been Nice", was presented at the Lantern in 1975. "I Do Not Like Thee, Doctor Fell" was his first full-length play. He recently wrote "Legs Eleven" for The Moving Theatre Company in the 1979 Dublin Theatre Festival. His latest play is "Canaries".
    He lives in Sandycove, County Dublin.

ACT ONE
SCENE ONE

A large, bare, third-storey room where the encounter group will meet. No furniture or trappings except for cushions scattered about and a tin bucket in the corner. Entrance door at left. Door to off-stage Contemplation Room at right. Window at back is bricked up. A locked box, containing a telephone with a lead-in wire, is fixed to the wall beside the entrance door.

It is evening — about 8. 00 p.m. Paddy — an old man in dungarees — is carefully sweeping the floor, quietly singing 'High Noon' to himself. Hold for ten seconds. Joe speculatively enters. He is about 25 — a nervous type, he carefully carries a travelling bag. He watches Paddy for a while. When he speaks, he stammers.

Joe	Ex . . . . Excuse me.
	(Paddy continues sweeping and singing, unnoticing).
Joe	I be . . . beg your pardon.
Paddy	Ah, good evening, sir — you're number one.
Joe	Nu . . . number one?
Paddy	Yeah, number one — the first to arrive. *(Pauses)* You are here for the Group thing-a-ma-gig, aren't you? The head shrinkers?
Joe	Miss Bernstein's Group Therapy Se. . . Session?
Paddy	The very one — I call them the head shrinkers. Are you here for that?
Joe	Yes.
Paddy	Well, find somewhere to sit, sunshine — they'll all be here in a minute.
	(Joe moves around. Paddy sweeps).
Joe	Are . . . are you here for Therapy as well?
Paddy	Me? Are you joking or something? Would I be sweeping up this kip if I was one of them? *(Mock officialdom).* I'm what's known as the Group Attendant — that's what I am. The Group Attendant.

Joe	Oh I see.
Paddy	Not my real job, of course. I'm really the caretaker of this whole building but, on a Saturday night, I become the Group Attendant. Do you get me?
Joe	Yes. *(Takes out cigarettes).* Smoke?
Paddy	What's that?
Joe	Wo . . . would you like a ci. . . ci. . . cig . . .
Paddy	Cigarette? No, never touch them, sunshine — bad for the 'oul bronchial tubes, you know. But thanks all the same.
Joe	Is it alright if I . . . ?
Paddy	Oh, fire ahead sunshine, fire ahead. Just watch the ash.
Joe	Oh yes.
Paddy	*(Placing the bucket).* Here, you can use that.
Joe	Oh thanks.
	(Paddy sweeps)
Paddy	What's the trouble anyway, sunshine? The nerves? The gargle? Women?
Joe	No, no, I'm just inter . . . inter . . . inter . . . I've just got reas . . reas . . . reasons . . .
Paddy	Reasons? Yeah, I understand. Well, I only hope they fix you up alright.
Joe	What are they like?
Paddy	What's that, sunshine?
Joe	I . . . I . . . was wo . . . wondering what are they like.
Paddy	What are they like? *(Laughs)* Ah, they're usually alright.
Joe	Are they?
Paddy	Yeah, they're alright . . . I suppose.
Joe	*(Quietly).* Just alright?
Paddy	*(Looking carefully at Joe).* Well, truthfully now, sunshine, I'll tell you what they're like, in my experience: they're not a bit like you — that's what they're like. Not your tyoe, if you understand.
Joe	No? Wh . . what's their type?
Paddy	I shouldn't be saying this but, in my opinion, Weirdos — that's the type. Give you an example — last week they had a fellow who thought he was Henry the Eighth. Seriously, really thought he was Henry the Eighth, Dirty 'oul bugger. A good boot in the arse is what he needed.
Joe	*(Laughing).* Go away?
Paddy	That's all he needed — a good runnin' boot in the arse.
Joe	So wh . . . what did they do for him?

6

Paddy	Ah now, there I leave you, sunshine. What they did for him is no concern of mine. I'm just the Group Attendant, you understand — I lock them in here, I go home, look at the telly, talk to the missus, read the paper, see how the nags went, put the chiselers to bed (if I can find them), come back here, bring in the grub, go home, have a kip, come back in the morning and turn them all loose. And what happens in the meantime is no concern of mine.
Joe	Oh, I see.
Paddy	And I still say you don't look the type. Truthfully, now, if I saw you outside, I'd be surprised to see you coming in here. I'm surprised to see you *in* here now.
Joe	Well, I was just cur . . . cur . . . curi . . .
Paddy	Curious?
Joe	Yes, Curious.
Paddy	Killed the cat, didn't it? Curiosity. Isn't that what they say? Curiosity killed the cat.
Joe	Yes.
Paddy	Ah, don't mind me, sunshine — I'm only talking. You'll be alright. You'll see. . .
	(A sudden commotion outside. Suzy Bernstein rushes in, carrying an attache case and clip-board. In her twenties, she speaks with a slick American accent, is alert — all action and efficiency. She is followed by Roger — in his twenties, exudes good breeding, is politely enthusiastic).
Suzy	Goddam cabs — Jesus no — taxis! I'll never get used to your expressions.
Roger	*(Laughing patronisingly).* The Great Divide, you know, — the little difference. Vive les petites differences.
Suzy	Right on, Roger. 'Evening Paddy.
Paddy	Good evening, Miss Bernstein. Just one arrived so far.
Suzy	Two. This is Roger — a comely nomad I encountered on the stairs. *(Checks clip-board).* Now, you are. . .?
Joe	Jo. . .Jo. . .Joe Fell.
Suzy	One name only — we all start equal. Right Joe, say hello to Roger — relax, relate, communicate. Blood brothers in embryo.
Roger	Hello, did you say your name was Fell?
Suzy	First names only, folks — it's a rule. *(Checks clip).*
Roger	Ah, but a simple lapsus lingua — slip of the tongue — from Joe You did say Fell?

Joe	Joe Fell.
Roger	Fell, Fell, Yes, *Doctor* Fell — that's it. Are you familiar with Martial?
Joe	Who?
Roger	Martial — the Spanish writer. First century.
Joe	No, I . . . don't think so.
Roger	With your name, you must know his Epigrammata?
Joe	No.
Roger	You don't know his "Non amo te, sabidi, nec possum dicere quare"?
Joe	*(Puzzled).* No.
Roger	Well, you should. Or at least the celebrated translation by Thomas Browne (1663 — 1704) — what was it now? Oh yes — "I do not like thee, Doctor Fell/ and why it is, I cannot tell/ I only know and know so well / I do not like thee, Doctor Fell" You've heard that before, surely?
Joe	No. . .I. . .I don't think so.
Roger	Oh, well it's quite well known.
Suzy	*(Writing on clip-board).* Joe and Roger, okay, We have one, two, three to come. A Peter, a Rita and a Maureen — beautiful Irish names. Everything A-OK, Paddy?
Paddy	Yes, Miss Bernstein — the soap and towels are inside and I've set the table. . .
Suzy	Fine, we'll just check that out. *(Leaves for other room with Paddy).* Don't run away, kids. . . be right back. *(Short, uncomfortable silence).*
Roger	Very efficient woman that.
Joe	Do . . . do you know her?
Roger	Oh no no no no no, just my considered — very considered — opinion.
Joe	Oh.
Roger	Opinion is the medium between knowledge and ignorance — do you agree?
Joe	What? Oh yes.
Roger	*(Thoughtfully)* Oh yes, ignorance and knowledge. . . *(Silence).*
Joe	She's an American, isn't she?
Roger	Mirabile, mirabile, Herr Doctor Fell — she is indeed. From Texaleto in Utah.
Joe	Utah? Arizona.
Roger	Pardon me?
Joe	Texaleto is in Ar. . .Arizona.

Roger	Arizona? No — Texaleto, Utah. The lady clearly said so.
Joe	I re. . . read in a book by Zane Gray that Texaleto was in Ar . . . Arizona.
Roger	Zane who?
Joe	Gray.
Roger	Gray? Gray? No.
Joe	He writes cowboy books.
Roger	Ha! No, Texaleto in the State of Utah — no doubt about it. She said so. *(Silence)*
Joe	Is this your first Th . . . Therapy here?
Roger	All life is a Therapy, Joe — but yes, this will be my first with Miss Bernstein.
Joe	You've been to others?
Roger	Oh, yes, the odyssey of self-discovery is a perpetual search: Berlin — very efficient, London — prissy, one in Rome — too emotional , Oslo was really excellent.
Joe	Yeah?
Roger	Touch therapy there. The flesh contact — a true discovery. Man to man, soul to soul, mind to mind. . . beautiful, beautiful. . . Apollos, Davids, Titans. . .bodies *homo antiqua virtute ac fide* . . . virtue and loyalty . . .
Joe	Is that where they all take off their clothes?
Roger	*(Loftily)* Yes, you could put it like that, I suppose.
Joe	I don't think they do that here.
Roger	You've been here before, then?
Joe	No.
Roger	Well then, how can you possibly assume. . .? *(Peter and Maureen enter. They are in their thirties — a sub-urban couple. Maureen carries a suitcase.)*
Peter	Hello there — the Suzy Bernstein Therapy Group?
Roger	*(Full of new enthusiasm)*. Yes, yes, entrez, entrez, abandon hope and all that . . . . face thy doom ye slaves of Rome. . .
Peter	Ah good — come along, love. Mind the step. Good girl.
Maureen	Oooh, a nice big room, isn't it?
Roger	I'm Roger, this is Joe — you must be Peter and, shall I guess, Rita?
Peter	I'm Peter alright — this is Maureen, my wife. Who's Rita?
Roger	I've no idea really.
Maureen	*(Looking around)* The window is all blocked up. *(Laughs)*

9

Peter	Then why did you say Rita?
Roger	Well, it had to be a Rita or a Maureen.
Maureen	*(Hearing her name)* Yes?
Peter	Why did it have to be a Rita or a Maureen?
Roger	Ah, the initial confusion of souls in search. My apologies — Miss Bernstein read out the names of those to come and there was a Rita and a Maureen. So I speculated that your wife was Rita.
Peter	No, she's Maureen.
Roger	Quite — my speculation was incorrect. Rita is the persona in absentia.
Peter	She's the what?
Roger	The missing one — the one to come.
Peter	Ah, I see — and that's how you knew I was Peter.
Maureen	No chairs though. Funny.
Roger	Exactly. And I'm Roger and this is Joe. *(These shake hands, muttering greetings)*
Peter	Maureen, say hello to Roger and Joe here. Come on now.
Maureen	How are you Roger.
Roger	I'm very well, Maureen — not Rita, eh? *(Shakes hands).*
Maureen	No, Maureen.
Joe	Hello.
Maureen	Hello Joe. *(Memorising names).* Roger and Joe. *(Suzy rushes in again, followed by Paddy)*
Suzy	. . . and dinner at 23 hundred hours on the dot and don't forget the phone check . . . oh, hi there, people — Peter and . . . Rita?
Roger/Peter	*Maureen!*
Suzy	You win a few and you lose a few — nice to see you. I'm Suzy, your Group Co-Ordinator for tonight, Okay? Right, just settle down, people — get acquainted while we wait for. . . eh. . . Rita. Relax, relate, communicate.
Peter	Will we put our suitcases in the other room. . .?
Suzy	Oh yeah, Jesus yeah. Suitcases. Now folks, suitcases, overnight bags, watches, clocks and all that stuff remain outside. Paddy'll put them in a closet just outside the door. All you need is a toilet bag — toothpaste and such-like. We divest ourselves of everything here — first our holdalls then our hang-ups. Get it?
Roger	*(Holding aloft a single toothbrush)* Voila.

Suzy	Ah-ha, been down this road before, eh Roger? Okay others, take what you need and give the rest to Paddy. *(Maureen rumages in the suitcase)*.
Joe	*(Weakly)* Is there a gentlem. . .gentlem. . .gentlemen's. . .?
Suzy	A which, Joe?
Joe	A jacks where I can. . .
Roger	I think he means the loo.
Suzy	Oh yeah, sorry Joe. Folks, the washroom, the kitchen and the Contemplation Room are all out here, okay? Great. *(Checks Clip-board again)* Going to have a really good session here tonight.
Peter	*(Watching Maureen)* Are they there, Maureen?
Maureen	Yes, I have them. *(Takes out a small toilet-bag)*.
Paddy	*(To Maureen)* I'll take that case, love.
Maureen	Oh, thank you very much *(Struggles with clips)*. It's rusty.
Joe	*(Going off into room)* I just want to get some stuff out of my bag. . .
Paddy	Fair enough, sunshine — I'll get yours later. *(To Maureen)*. That's grand, love *(Leaves)*
Roger	Splendid weather today, Peter.
Peter	For the time of year, Roger.
Roger	You like the sun, I can see. Nice tan. All over?
Peter	Ah, I don't bother too much — got most of that on the building site. I like the summer though.*(Quietly)* Women, you know.
Roger	Pardon?
Peter	You know, women — flashes all over the place — frilly dresses, cheesecloth, transparent . . .oh-ho, it all happens in the summer. Randy weather.
Roger	Oh yes.
Peter	Good for a bit of yabadaba-doooooo.
Roger	*(Coldly)* Yes, quite.
Peter	Never mention that to the wife, though. A quiet flash is what you want. Nothing like the sly flash. . .
Roger	My summer is the body. The heat. Therapeutic.
Peter	Thera-what?
Roger	You know — good for the metabolism.
Maureen	*(To Peter)* He's nice — he called me love. Twice.
Peter	Who did?
Maureen	The man with the bags.

Peter	*(Looking after Paddy)* Did he? *(To Suzy)* Who's that man, Miss Bernstein?
Suzy	Suzy, please. That's Paddy — the Group Attendant. Joe? Are you okay? Find it alright?
Joe	*(Arriving back)* Yes, I'm fin. . .fin. . . I'm grand.
Suzy	Good. Paddy? One more bag here. *(Checking names again)* Got to get this show on the road fast. Paddy'll take that bag, Joe. Okay people, take a look in here, familiarise yourselves while we wait for. . .eh. . .Rita. Paddy! One bag here. Paddy! Paddy!
	(Suzy, Roger, Maureen and Peter leave for Contemplation Room, Joe waits)
Paddy	*(Running in)* Jaysus, such shouting — she'll have me as bad as the rest of you. Oh, no offence, sunshine — how's it going so far?
Joe	Oh grand.
Paddy	Any sign of Henry the Eighth?
Joe	No — wh. . .where are you putting my bag?
Paddy	*(Laughs)* What have you got in it? A bomb? Or just a few sticks of gelignite? Do I hear it ticking?
Joe	No. . .it's ju. . just that I got a loan of that ba. .bag and I do. . .don't want to lo. . lo. . loose
Paddy	Ah don't worry about it, sunshine — I'm putting it in the closet out here. It'll be safe and sound. You'll be locked up in here, the bags will be waiting out there and I'll be watching the telly at home. Gas set-up, isn't it?
Joe	Do you know where Tex. . .Tex. . .Texaleto is?
Paddy	A pub, is it?
Joe	No, a place.
Paddy	Texaleto? No, where is it?
Joe	It's in Arizona.
Paddy	Go way.
Joe	Yes. Wonder what happens here next.
Paddy	*(Sternly)* Ah, a few orgies — roaring and screaming — running around naked. . .
Joe	*(Sternly)* Do you think so?
Paddy	I'm only codding you, sunshine. Truthfully, I haven't a clue and I care less. I see nothing, I hear nothing (because the whole kip is sound- proof) and I ask no questions — and that suits me.
	(Rita cautiously enters. She is 50/60. Carries a handbag)

12

Rita	Hello.
Paddy	*(To Joe)* Jaysus, Queen Victoria *(To Rita)* Yes madam?
Rita	My name is Rita. Is this the Suzy Bernstein Group Therapy Session?
Paddy	Indeed it is, madam — come in. Do you have a suitcase?
Rita	A suitcase?
Paddy	A suitcase.
Rita	No, just my handbag. . .But you may take my coat.
Paddy	That's grand, madam. Make yourself at home — Miss Bernstein is in the next room. *(To Joe)* Hope that she doesn't take anything else off!
Rita	Thank you very much.
Paddy	Don't mention it, madam *(Leaves with Joe's bag and Rita's coat)*
Rita	A very polite young man.
Joe	*(Looking after Paddy)* Young? *(To Rita)* He's just the Group Assistant, I think. Just locks up and brings in the food and helps Miss Bernstein.
Rita	Oh pity. Are you one of the group?
Joe	Yes, my name's Joe Fell. . .no, ju. . .just Joe. There are three other people. They're in there with Miss Bernstein. We're supposed to look around.
Rita	Not really much to see, is there? Do you like cats?
Joe	Cats? Well, they're alright. I had one once. It died.
Rita	Oh poor thing. My husband loved cats. We had twelve of them, you know. We called them after the Twelve Apostles. Judas was our favourite *(Pause)* I miss him very much.
Joe	Wh. . .what happened to him?
Rita	He was savaged by dogs.
Joe	That often happens to cats.
Rita	No no, Judas is still alive. It was my husband who was savaged by dogs.
Joe	Oh.
Rita	Yes, I have a very bad heart condition ever since. Are you a doctor?
Joe	A doctor? No, not really.
Rita	Pity. I don't like the idea of being locked up in here without a doctor. I get turns, you know. That's why I always carry my handbag with me. All my tablets.
Joe	Ah, I see.
Rita	I get depressed, you know — since my husband died. I miss

	him very much. How long is your wife dead?
Joe	She. . .she's not dead.
Rita	Oh, you're so lucky.
Joe	No, I. . .I mean I'm not married.
Rita	Ah, pity. We could have shared the emotion of loss. Loss is a terrible thing, you know.

(Suzy and Roger return)

Roger	. . . do you know that Hegel wrote that this inanimate reaction is still relatively unimportant in terms of personality and conscience. . .
Suzy	Right-on, Roger. . . .Ah, at last — Rita. It is Rita, isn't it?
Rita	Yes, are you Miss Bernstein?
Suzy	Suzy, please. Good to see you. Now can we get going. Oh, this is Roger. Peter and Maureen are looking over the Contemplation Room — right out there — and Joe, I see, you have met. Paddy? Paddy? Paddy!
Paddy	*(Running in)* Yes, Miss Bernstein?
Suzy	Everything in order?
Paddy	Yes, Miss Bernstein.
Suzy	A quick check of names — Joe, Roger, Rita here; Peter and Maureen outside . . . . Great, fine. Peter, Maureen! Come in here a moment. *(Peter and Maureen appear)* Okay, now we are all set for our great blast-off into our own world. All set to batten down the hatches, lock up the coop. Paddy is going to seal us all in and he won't appear until 23 hundred hours with our dinner.
Rita	What time?
Suzy	Twenty-three hundred hours, Rita.
Peter	That's nine o'clock, Maureen.
Suzy	No, eleven, Peter, eleven. Twenty-three hundred. Right?
Peter	Yes, yes, eleven. Eleven o'clock, Maureen.
Rita	Eleven o'clock.
Suzy	Okay. Apart from Paddy's arrival and until he releases us in the morning, we shall live in search — in search of inner knowledge, of ourselves and of others. We have no windows, as you have noticed, the room is soundproof and our only connection with the outside world (in case of emergencies) is a telephone which is sealed in that box, right over there.
Rita	Where?
Suzy	Right over there, Rita — just for emergencies. *(Laughs)* No phoning loved ones — we will be the whole world.

Roger	Ah, the sensory stimulation of incarceration.
Rita	My husband is dead — he was savaged by dogs.
Suzy	Fine. So let's take a last look at the outside world, people. In a moment, we will become a family with its own laws, rules and we'll be responsible to no-one. It is a great moment, folks, and in Encounter Groups we have a symbolic way of imposing this upon our minds. It is our first Group ritual — the long farewell, the beginning of our journey into the unknown chasms of the mind.
Roger	Beautiful . . . beautiful. . .
Paddy	*(To Joe)* Here it comes now.
Suzy	So, as a simple symbolism of our being reborn, let's all wave goodbye to Paddy as he returns to his world and we withdraw into our own. It is our rebirth, our appearance from the womb of convention, of discipline, of hypocrisy, of bureaucracy. So wave goodbye to Paddy. This is very symbolic, people. Now goodbye Paddy.
Paddy	Jaysus!
Roger	Ciao, Paddy. Ciao.
Peter	Bye-bye, Paddy.
Suzy	That's it, folks — wave.
Maureen	Goodbye, love.
Paddy	Good luck, sunshine.
	(Paddy leaves, door is locked. Silence)
Peter	*(To Maureen)* There was no need for that.
Maureen	For what?
Peter	For that 'goodbye love'.
Maureen	I was just saying goodbye, for Heaven's sake.
Roger	We did this in Oslo, you know.
Joe	Yeah?
Rita	Such a nice young man.
Suzy	*(Springs to life again. Goes to telephone box. Pulls a long string from her inside her shirt on which hangs the key to the box)* Okay, fine. Right people, you just relax, relate, communicate while I check the phone here. *(Opens box. Dials number)* Four. . . Zero. . .Zero. . .Seven. . .
Peter	*(To Rita)* We didn't really meet — I'm Peter and this is my wife, Maureen.
Rita	How very nice. Are you a doctor?
Suzy	Hello Paddy? Paddy? Can you hear me okay?
Peter	A doctor? No — do I look like a doctor?

15

Maureen	*(Laughing loudly)* You do, dear — really, you do.
Suzy	Okay Paddy, you try now. *(Replaces phone)* Phone's okay out, people. Paddy'll ring in now to check.
Roger	Excellent organisation. First class.
Suzy	Thank you, Roger.
Rita	*(To Maureen)* Are *you* a doctor?
Maureen	Oh deary me. *(Laughs)* No, I'm not.
Peter	Get a grip on yourself, Maureen. *(To Rita)* No, she's not — but *you* look like a doctor, Rita. Are you? *(Phone rings)*
Suzy	*(Shouting)* Hello Paddy. Yes Fine. You're loud and clear.
Rita	Oh no, I'm not a doctor — my husband's best friend was a doctor. He was savaged by dogs, you know.
Suzy	That's fine, Paddy. . .
Peter	Dogs? Hey, did you hear that, Roger?
Roger	Yes, the phone is working.
Peter	No, Rita's husband's best friend was savaged by dogs. He was a doctor.
Roger	How absolutely dreadful. Did he die?
Rita	No no, he's still alive — *he* loves dogs. It was my husband who was savaged. He loved cats. I miss him so much.
Suzy	That's great, Paddy. Okay fine. 'Bye Paddy.
Peter	I thought you said it was your husband's best friend. . ?
Suzy	Okay people, now look here. The phone is fine and I'm locking it with this key and I'm keeping the key around my neck like this. *(Puts key back inside her shirt)* So, if I drop dead — ha ha — you'll know where to find it. Okay?
Peter	*(Quietly to Roger)* I wouldn't mind searching for it. . . . . yabadaba-dooooooo.
Rita	Yes, I've had a heart condition ever since.
Roger	Very understandable Rita —cela va sans dire, as they say.
Suzy	Fine. Right. Now let's get this show on the road. Everyone sit on the cushions for a moment while I explain a few things.
Rita	Do I have to sit down?
Suzy	Just for a moment, Rita.
Maureen	I'll sit here beside Joe — he looks lonely. Hello Joe.
Peter	Sit here, Maureen — beside me.
Maureen	I just thought that Joe . . .
Peter	Joe's alright where he is.
Maureen	Very well, he just looked lonely, that's all. I'll sit here beside Peter, Joe.
Joe	I. . .I don't mind. . .

16

Suzy	Wherever you like, people —just settle down.
Rita	I think I'll sit beside Joe — he likes cats.
Roger	Ah, relationships building up already, Suzy. I'll stay neutral.
Suzy	Right-on, Roger. Okay, all settle down.
Rita	I have to be careful. It's my heart, you know.
Suzy	Okay, we're all comfortable? Right, now let's be quiet for a moment. Listen to that silence. Close your eyes and listen. Right? Feel that silence spreading over each of us like a heavy mantle, binding us together like a mother's arms, bringing us close like a family. And at the end of this session, we *will* be like a family — a new family. Now, we are children, new to the world, on the first day of our recreation. We are all honesty, we have no masks, no inhibitions, no reason to feel indoctrinated, nothing to conform to — we are free. We are naked, naked to reach out and explore, to ask, to receive, to belong. . . .
Rita	I like the quiet, Joe — don't you?
Suzy	Just let it linger, folks.
Roger	Ah yes. . . ah yes. . .
Suzy	*(Softly)* Anyone want to say anything at this point in time? Express some feeling? Some hope? Anything.
Roger	I feel. . .I wonder. . .I want. . .
Suzy	Yes, Roger?
Roger	I wonder if it's better to live alone or to die alone.
Suzy	Fine Roger — that's a good vibration.
Rita	I wonder if my husband hears me.
Suzy	Fine, Rita.
Roger	Better perhaps to live happily or to die happily. *(Maureen sniggers)*
Suzy	Maureen? You got a vibration? An impulse?
Maureen	No. Nothing.
Peter	Get a grip on yourself, for Heaven's sake.
Rita	Can. . .can he see me. . .?
Suzy	Fine Rita, we'll probe that.
Joe	How long is a piece of string. . . *(Maureen laughs)*
Roger	Is it better to see the world or to live blindly in its image. . .
Suzy	Fine, fine. . .anyone else? Anyone? Great, okay. Now, very quietly, let us try our first Group exercise. We have been hushed together, tuning our minds — now let us touch. This, people is a group exercise that accelerates the normal pursuit

17

	of discovery. So, let us reach out and touch. Let us try this. . .
Roger	*(Reaching towards Peter)* Yes yes yes. . .
Suzy	No Roger, hold it — not just touching whom we know, but in the darkness of search.
Roger	Oh yes, of course — I had forgotten.
Suzy	*(Rises)* So, easy now, for this initiation I'm going to turn off the light for a moment and we shall stand and move and touch, okay?
Rita	Do I have to stand up again?
Suzy	Just to move around quietly. Okay, let's go. Everyone ready? Okay. *(Lights out)* Move around now. Touch.
Rita	I can't find my handbag. . .
Suzy	Quietly please, silently — okay? Move, touch, move, touch — we are people, right? Crucibles of energy, of hopes, dreams, promises, problems . . . reach out . . .touch. . .
Rita	Ah, I have it. . .
Maureen	*(Giggles)* Is that you, Peter?
Peter	Oooooops, sorry there. . .
Rita	Where did I leave my tablets. . . they don't seem to be. . .
Suzy	Slowly, slowly — concentrate. That's it — reach out, touch. . . .
Maureen	*(Sudden scream)* Who's that?!
Peter	Maureen! Are you alright?
Maureen	*(Scream and laugh)* Who was that?!
Rita	Who screamed?
Peter	Maureen, where are you?
Rita	Suzy, someone screamed. . .
Maureen	Peter? Peter?
	(Lights on. Maureen is beside Peter and Roger. Joe is alone. Rita is searching her handbag)
Peter	What happened, Maureen? What the hell happened?
Suzy	It's okay, folks — all sit down now . . .
Peter	Maureen, what happened?
Maureen	*(Looking around)* Someone touched . . . me *(Giggles)*
Peter	Where? Who? For God's sake who?
Rita	Ah, I found my tablets — here they are here.
Suzy	It's okay, folks — just an exercise . . . settle down now . . .
Peter	*(To Roger)* Did you . . . did you touch my wife?
Roger	For heaven's sake, I assure you that I did nothing improper . . .
Maureen	It's alright Peter — it wasn't anything.
Peter	Then why did you scream? What the hell happened? *(To Joe)* My God, did you . . . ?

18

Joe	What?
Suzy	People, people, people, please. This is supposed to be a Touch Therapy . . .
Roger	Yes, of course it is.
Peter	If I find the person who tried to . . to . . to . . .
Maureen	Come on, Peter, it was nothing. Don't make a scene.
Suzy	Just all sit down, folks. Okay, Roger . . . Peter, please . . .
Rita	Do I have to sit down again?
Peter	You'd better all be careful . . .
Suzy	Fine, Peter, please sit down. Yes, Rita, sit down please for the moment.
Peter	You sit down beside me, Maureen.
Maureen	*(Annoyed)* I am I am I am I am.
Suzy	Okay now, just a bit of friction there — and that is good. That's very good for the session. We need that. Now, let's all open up to each other. Let's just talk. Now, who wants to start? *(Silence)* Okay, I'm Suzy Bernstein, I come from Texaleto in the State of . . . eh . . . Utah and my greatest wish is for the success of this Session. I want to admit that I'm nervous, anxious for us all. I speak honestly — and I want all of you to open up to me and to each other . . . in such honesty, that, in the end we will all become close and intimate and understanding. Now, who'll begin?
Roger	I am Roger . . .
Suzy	Fine Roger — you just want to talk to us, right? Okay.
Roger	I am a name, a body — you see my form, my face, my physique. But I am also an energy, a nebulous undefinable energy. I am me — yet, to me, I am a stranger. I hear echoes — echoes of my own voice repeating back to me everything that I doubt. I see . . . I *am* animal . . . I see the fox that waits and watches, I see the horse that stands and prances, I . . . I see the elephant that moves in a great, strong sadness . . . and I am all of these. I see . . .
Rita	Cats?
	(Maureen laughs. Peter looks at her).
Roger	Pardon me?
Rita	Do you see cats?
Roger	Cats? No, I don't . . . I'm trying to say that I relate my search to the animal, to the consciousless beings . . . I resent . . . — yet admire — their freedom, their . . .
Rita	You must be a vet.

Roger	A vet? No, I'm an artist, a seeker — a seeker frustrated by the belief that life, however beautiful, is a terminal disease.
Rita	You should be a vet. We used to take our cats to a vet. He loved animals . . . and terminal diseases.
Roger	May I . . . may I speak honestly? May I give a here-and-now reaction to the family? We used to do this in Oslo.
Suzy	Sure Roger, just open up. We are all here to listen with great honesty and to help. We are, as you say, your family.
Roger	Thank you, Suzy. Well, I see a great resentment towards me. . .
Maureen	Oh no . . .
Roger	Yes I do, Maureen: from Rita with whom I have great difficulty in relating but to whom I want to relate so much, from Joe whom I do not understand because of his silence, from Peter, who I feel, suspects me . . .
Maureen	Oh no — that's not true . . .
Peter	I'll handle this, Maureen. I . . . I . . . eh . . . I don't suspect you and. . . and I'm sorry if I shouted at you. *(To Suzy)* Is that alright?
Suzy	Great, great, Peter. We had a misunderstanding there and we've conquered it. That's very good for the Session.
Peter	To be honest, I know that Maureen is highly-strung and that, really, is why we're here. Isn't that right Maureen?
Maureen	Yes Peter.
Rita	I feel that way since my husband died. I take tablets. Yoy should take tablets too, Maureen.
Peter	No, I decided against that. To be committed to one's work is more important. Isn't that right, Maureen?
Maureen	Yes, Peter.
Roger	That's true, Peter — I find consolation in my painting, in the arts, in my exploration of the human body . . .
Maureen	Peter builds.
Roger	Peter builds?
Suzy	Who? Peter who?
Maureen	Peter — he builds.
Peter	I'm a building contractor.
Suzy	Oh, I get it — you're in real estate.
Peter	Specialise in select bungalows. Apollo Homes. Exclusive design . . .
Roger	How artistic. Absolutely beautiful.
Peter	Thank you. All my bungalows can be built to individual specification — use only quality jig-assembled component

	parts, all cavity walls; anti-rot, infestation-free timber . . . all supplied to individual taste . . .
Rita	Very interesting. Is the market good?
Maureen	He has no trouble selling . . .
Peter	The new wave of buyer in the private sector demands this select, different, individual type and . . .
Roger	. . . and you build them. How absolutely magnificent.
Maureen	Peter designed and built our own home . . .
Roger	A bungalow?
Peter	Of course — this one my own, exclusive design. Apollo-plus, I call it.
Roger	Ah, Apollo . . .
Maureen	You'd love this kitchen, Rita — we had it panelled in pine . . .
Peter	. . . all natural wood units . . .
Maureen	. . . a copper canopy over the hob unit of the cooker . . .
Peter	Split-level cooker, Maureen . . .
Maureen	And the wall fabric of the . . .
Peter	The wall fabric of the T.V. lounge-cum-study was my special choice — hessian. Really hard-wearing yet visually attractive. . .
Roger	It sounds absolutely magnificent . . .
Maureen	Four bedrooms . . .
Peter	Bathroom en suite with the main one, drawingroom lounge with built-in bookshelves and a picture window, dining area off.
Maureen	. . . T.V. lounge and study . . .
Peter	I said that, Maureen. Ground floor split-level, of course, insulated tiled roofs,
Maureen	. . . utility room. . .
Peter	. . . separate WC's, cloakroom.
Rita	Children's room?
Peter	A what?
Rita	A children's room.
Peter	No, we don't have any children.
Rita	Ah pity. If my husband and I had children, we would never have had cats. He said that before he was savaged . . .
Suzy	Would you like to have children, Maureen?
Maureen	Well, to be perfectly honest, soon after we married, I. . .
Peter	We decided not to have any children.
Suzy	Did you really? Don't you like. . . ?
Peter	We decided not to have any children.
Suzy	But you do like children?
Peter	*(Sternly)* We just decided not to have any.

21

Suzy	Oh, I see.
Maureen	Yes, we just decided not to. . . have any children. *(Short silence)*
Suzy	Hey Joe, we haven't heard from you yet.
Joe	Me?
Roger	*(Laughing)* I know he reads cowboy books because he told me that.
Rita	He isn't a doctor — he told *me* that.
Roger	He's Doctor Fell — aren't you, Joe?
Rita	No, he isn't a doctor. He told me so.
Maureen	Can we guess what Joe is. . . can we?
Peter	Well, see what Suzy thinks . . .
Suzy	Why not? That would be a good exercise in speculation — our Session must be completely flexible, right? So why not — I'm sure we'll discover how wrong we can be in speculation. Okay by you, Joe?
Joe	I. . .I. . .I don't mind.
Suzy	Great. Any guesses?
Roger	*(Thoughtfully)* I would say that you have a desk job, Joe. I would speculate that you are an accountant, perhaps, or a. . .
Peter	No no, never. I deal with accountants in my business. No, Joe works with his hands — am I right, Joe?
Maureen	Don't say, Joe, let me guess. You are a carpenter, aren't you?
Rita	One of my husband's best friends knew a carpenter, but I can't say what he looked like because I never met him.
Suzy	Well Joe — how are we doing? *(Joe shakes his head)*
Roger	Wait — a second guess.
Maureen	No, that's not fair — one guess, Roger.
Suzy	Shall we let him have a second guess, family?
Maureen	Well, alright. . .
Suzy	Okay with all? Okay, Roger, the family grants you a second guess.
Roger	I say that Joe could be a traveller — a salesman. . .
Peter	No, no, never, I know salesmen in my business. Not a salesman, never.
Suzy	Joe?
Joe	You're all wr. . . wrong
Suzy	Did I not say so, people? Now we know how false it is to judge by appearance. So what are you, Joe?
Joe	*(Stammering badly)* I am a ra. . ra. . radio ann. . ann. . annou-

ncer. I re. . re. . .read the news on the ra. . radio.
(Silence)

Peter	You're joking! *(To Maureen)* He reads the news like that!
Rita	Really — do you?
Maureen	*(Laughing)* Oh, we're sorry, Joe — but do you honestly? I mean, can you. . . well, what I mean is. . is. . .I never heard you.
Peter	Reads the news!
Maureen	I really never heard him.
Rita	I don't like the news — it's all so depressing and my heart is not strong since my husband was. . .
Roger	No, this is interesting. I too find it hard to accept, but it *is* possible.
Peter	Is it?
Roger	Oh yes, I have known people with a, you know, a speech impediment who can actually speak quite fluently if they are. . .
Joe	*(Shouts)* Well, I don't .
Roger	You don't? You mean when you read the news, you don't stammer. . . ?
Joe	I don't read the news.
Suzy	Joe, you said you read the news on the radio.
Joe	Well, I don't. I can't read the ne. . .ne. . .news.
Peter	*(Angry)* Then what are you? This isn't a game. We're all trying to be honest here.
Roger	I said what I was — I was being quite honest.
Rita	So was I.
Peter	Well, what are you?
Maureen	Perhaps Joe would prefer not to tell us.
Peter	Not tell us? Then what's he going to do? Just sit there and listen? Of course he'll have to tell us.
Roger	Yes Joe, of course you must open up and. . .
Peter	Come on, tell us.
Roger	We are your family, remember.
Joe	*(Quietly)* I'm a trans-Atlantic pilot.
Rita	A what? What did he say?
Peter	He said he was a pilot.
Joe	*(Louder)* And I'm a rat-catcher.
Peter	A what? — you're a what?
Joe	And I'm a doctor and I'm a thinker. . .
Peter	Wait a minute!

23

Joe	*(Louder)* And I'm a cat-lover and a builder of exclusive bung-alows *(Shouts louder)* and I . . .I'm the man who puts the cracks into cream crackers and the. . .the. . .
Suzy	Hold it, Joe. . .
Joe	. . .and I'm the promised Messiah, I'm the Riddle of the Sphinx, I. . .I'm the Salt of the Earth, I. . .I'm Rocky Marciano . . . I'm . . . I'm everything that crawls, flies, walks, shuffles, staggers, . . .I'm . . .I'm . . . I'm . . *(Silence)*
Peter	Oh my God. *(Maureen laughs)* Shut up, Maureen — get a grip on yourself.
Suzy	*(Controlled)* Joe, do you want to tell us? *(Silence)* Would you like to tell me? Or anyone? *(Silence)* What would you like to do?
Joe	I'd like to go to the jacks.
Suzy	The what, Joe?
Roger	He means the loo.
Suzy	Oh sure, sure. You know where it is. You don't have to ask. It's okay, Joe — go ahead. It's okay. *(Joe leaves)*
Peter	My God, are we safe in here with him? Are you alright Maureen?
Maureen	Yes, of course I am.
Peter	And you wanted to sit beside him. My God!
Maureen	I just said that to be sociable.
Peter	Sociable? With him? Well, you just sit there now.
Maureen	I *am* sitting here.
Rita	He was shouting — I don't like shouting. My husband would never shout.
Suzy	Okay, Okay — now how do we react? That's the point now, people. This is great for the Session. How can we help — what does the family see?
Roger	I see a great confusion — a mixture of blues and yellows, jagged lines. I see great layers emerging. Dostoyevsky says 'He who has a predilection for abstract deduction is ready to distort the truth for his own advantage' I am warned by this and I try to see. . .
Peter	I see a nut case! We're not safe locked in here with him!
Rita	He said he wasn't a doctor and then he said he was . . .
Roger	A real Doctor Fell perhaps — 'I do not like thee Doctor Fell, and why it is I cannot tell . . .'

24

Peter	I can tell why I don't like him — he's nuts!
Suzy	Look people, we can help — we must remember that. For the sake of the Session, we must try to understand to console, to relate, to. . . *(Joe enters)*. . . Oh Joe, come in. You okay?
Joe	*(Sits beside Rita)* Yes, I'm grand. I want to apologise.
Suzy	That's okay, Joe. Is it okay, people?
Roger	Indeed it is.
Joe	I'm very sorry.
Suzy	Don't worry, Joe — we can sort everything out. We all make mistakes, but with honesty and openness, the Session solves everything. So don't worry about it.
Peter	*(To Maureen)* It's alright now — don't worry.
Joe	I'm an electrician.
Rita	Ah, that's nice.
Peter	It's your current occupation! Get it? Current occupation — electrician.
Suzy	Good joke, Peter.
Joe	*(Smiling, relaxed)* Yes, that's good.
Roger	Joe, would you like to tell us exactly what you do — or would you prefer. . . ?
Joe	No no — I sit in a little office, at a brown desk and wait for the phone to ring for people to tell me that their per. . .percolator won't work or their toaster is broken and they can't have their breakfast. . .
Roger	Yes, I understand. . .
Joe	. . . or that their electric blanket won't get warm and that they can't sleep or that their shaver or their hairdryer won't work and they can't go out — and then I get into my little red van, drive over to them and fix whatever is wrong. That's all.
Suzy	That's great, Joe. Fine.
Roger	Ah, you work at night, then?
Joe	Week on, week off — yes.
Maureen	And you like your work?
Joe	It's interesting, sometimes.
Peter	Especially when you've got to fix an electric blanket, eh? Chance of a bit of yabadaba- dooooo.
Maureen	Peter! Don't be rude!
Peter	I'm not rude — it's a joke.
Joe	No, nothing like that.
Maureen	Of course not. Joe's not like that.

25

Roger	So there we are. Quod erat demonstrandum.
Suzy	Do you want to say something to Joe, Rita?
Rita	Yes — you're not a doctor then, are you?
Joe	No, I told you — I'm a pilot.
Peter	Holy Christ!
	(Silence)
Suzy	*(Controlled)* A pilot, Joe? I thought you said that you were an electrician?
Joe	Oh yes, I'm sorry — I'm an electrician. Not a pilot. Or a doctor.
Suzy	Okay, people — great. We've broken the ice, right? We all know each other a little better now, right? We've had a sudden sharing in a here-and-now situation, we've got some great reaction, we've sorted it out and that has brought us closer. Yet, we still wear masks, don't we? Some of us, I feel, are still showing a face to the world. So why don't we try our second Therapy exercise — and just regard each other for a moment. . .
Roger	Ah yes, we did this in Oslo. This is good.
Rita	Do I have to stand up again?
Suzy	Just for a moment, Rita — then we'll break for private communication. So will we try it? Just stand up, don't say a word, don't touch — just stare each other in the face. Get it? We call it eye-balling in the States *(Suzy stands up)*
Peter	Are you going to turn off the light again?
Suzy	No Peter, we'll leave the light on for this. Let's try it, slowly. *(All stand)*
Roger	Super. Hello Peter.
Suzy	Silently, please. Don't touch — just look.
Roger	Oh yes, of course.
	(All move around — staring each other)
Suzy	Let that look linger, folks. Move around, Peter — that's it. Gaze down into the soul. Don't hide anything. Just relax and let your eyes communicate *(Pause)* Quietly now. Great. Feel that silent discovery. . .
	(As they finish, Joe and Maureen stand gazing at each other)
Peter	Eh, Maureen. . . ?
Suzy	It's okay, Peter.
	(All watch in silence)
Peter	Maureen. . . .?
Roger	Shhhhhhhhhh. . . . . .
Rita	They look nice, don't they?

Roger	They're searching the hidden chasms of the mind. . .
Suzy	Quiet please — let them discover. . . .
Peter	Maureen. . . . ?
Suzy	Easy Peter — let them be. . .
Peter	*(Shouts)* Maureen, for God's sake. *(Disengages them)*
	(To Joe) What the hell are you at? This is my wife, you know.
Suzy	Hey Peter, easy — this is an exercise in discovery.
Peter	Well, I tell you what I discovered — he can't be trusted.
	Not with the truth and not with my wife. My God, Maureen!
Maureen	I'm sorry, Peter — I didn't hear you.
Peter	How bloody convenient — as usual.
Maureen	Now Peter, don't start that.
Peter	I didn't start it — you started it.
Roger	It's just an exercise, Peter — a discovery.
Peter	Well, ask him what *he* discovered.
Suzy	Joe?
Joe	What?
Suzy	Peter asks what you discovered.
Joe	*(Pause)* That I can't be trusted . . . at all.
Maureen	*(Laughs)* Oh deary me . . .
Peter	Get a grip on yourself, for God's sake.
Roger	Well, I discovered in Rita a great sadness. A blue — yes, a blue. It helps me to relate to her now. I see a great loss and I feel a need to reach out to her . . .
Rita	Do you really? I've had this great sadness since . . .
Joe	. . . he was savaged by dogs.
Rita	Yes, that's right, Joe.
Suzy	See? The layers are being stripped away, people. We've had our first general symposium — now it's time for private communication. We are now free to do as we please. We can sit here and develop our relationships or we can retire to the Contemplation Room. We are free for a while — get it?
Joe	What time is it?
Suzy	Time doesn't count here, Joe. Why do you ask?
Joe	No . . . No reason.
Suzy	Fine. We'll all reassemble before dinner okay?
Roger	Would you like to sit here with me, Rita?
Rita	Oh yes — did I tell you about my husband?
Peter	I want to talk to you, Maureen — privately.
Maureen	For Heaven's sake, Peter!
Peter	Yes, for Heaven's sake!

Suzy	Joe, are you going to join us?
Joe	*(Stands up)* Eh . . . no.
Peter	What are you going to do now?
Joe	*(Moves towards Contemplation Room)* I think I'll just con-template . . .
Peter	My God . . .!

Lights out. End of Scene One, Act One.

SCENE TWO

(When lights come up, Roger, Maureen, Suzy and Rita are talking. Peter is examining the walls. Joe is still in the Contemplation Room).

Roger	Ah, but the wish to be one's self does not occur — for only self known is empty and must be filled from the outside.
Maureen	Oh Roger, a bit slower, please. You say that we prefer to be someone other than ourselves?
Suzy	To be a pseudonym, you mean.
Roger	Yes, that too — Van Den Haag says that we long to impersonate, to get a name — better to be a pseudonym than to remain nameless; better a borrowed character than none; better to regard ourselves. . .
Peter	That's a load of rubbish.
Suzy	Sorry Peter — what was that?
Peter	*(Tapping the wall)* That plaster coat — covers a lot of sloppy work. . .
Suzy	Really?
Peter	No buyer would touch that nowadays — all very fine as a hotch-potch job, but to the select buyer — no.
Maureen	Yes, that's true, Peter.
Roger	As I was saying, de-individualisation should not be viewed as a grim, deliberate or coercive process — it is always, as in all. . .
Peter	And whoever bricked up that window should be shot.
Rita	Shot?

Suzy	Okay folks, we can leave it there for a moment — time for our next Session before dinner.
Roger	*(To Maureen)* It's simply a conclusion that, of real identity, we have no measure . . . .
Peter	If I put up a wall like that, I wouldn't sell. . .
Suzy	Okay fine — that's it for the present. Joe? Joe? *(Silence)* Would you come out now, Joe — we're having a General Session. Joe?
Peter	What the hell is he doing there, anyway?
Rita	I'd forgotten about Joe.
Roger	He's probably contemplating. . .
Peter	Contemplating what?
Joe	*(Appears)* Sor . . . sorry. I don't have my toothbrush.
Roger	Your toothbrush?
Joe	I'll have to get it out of my bag when Pa. . .Paddy opens the door.
Suzy	I thought you had one, Joe.
Roger	Yes, you did have one — I saw it.
Rita	Yes, I saw it too. It was green.
Peter	No, that was mine. Mine is green. Maureen's is orange.
Rita	*(To Roger)* Oranges are good for you — they contain calcium.
Suzy	Have you mislaid it, Joe?
Joe	No.
Roger	Then where is it?
Joe	It's in my bag. I'll have to get it when Pa. . .Paddy opens the door. *(Silence)*
Suzy	Look Joe, we can sort this out — we've been sorting lots of things out while you've been in there — haven't we, family? *(General agreement)* Now, what colour was it?
Joe	Black.
Peter	Black? A black toothbrush? I never saw anyone with a black toothbrush.
Roger	It was a primary colour, I think — I think I remember a yellow one.
Maureen	Yes yes — it was yellow. I remember because yellow is so near to orange and mine is orange and Peter's is pink.
Peter	No, mine is green.
Maureen	No, pink — your's is pink.
Peter	It's green, Maureen — I know the colour of my own bloody toothbrush.

29

Rita	Mine is blue. I like blue — it's restful.
Roger	Depends on the shade, Rita. A sky blue is rather pleasant.
Rita	That's what mine is — sky blue. It's very pleasant.
Maureen	Shall we all look for Joe's toothbrush then?
Peter	Look for it? Why?
Maureen	For fun — what else?
Suzy	Good idea — that's co-operation within the family. Come oh, Peter.
Peter	This is stupid — bloody stupid — looking for his. . . his tooth-brush. *(All stand)*
Roger	What colour are we looking for?
Maureen	Ah, that's the game. I say yellow, Joe says black, Rita says green.
Peter	Mine is green.
Suzy	Okay then, we'll give it two minutes of hard searching, people. Hard searching *(All begin to search)* Our whole session is a search, right?
Roger	*(From Contemplation Room)* Nothing in the bathroom — no blacks at all. . .
Rita	*(Lifting cushions)* I wish I could search more — I have to be careful, you know.
Roger	Just try a little — leave no stone unturned . . .
Maureen	. . .And no turn unstoned. . . .
Suzy	*(Laughing)* Come on, all try harder. . .
Maureen	*(Sing)* Come out little toothbrush, show your colour, Come out little toothbrush. . . *(Un-noticed, Joe takes a white toothbrush from his pocket and holds it aloft)*
Suzy	Come on, Peter — search. . .
Rita	I thought I saw it. . .no, it was nothing. . .
Suzy	One minute to go, folks and then we quit. . .
Maureen	No no, we'll find it. . .
Peter	*(Seeing Joe)* Hey, what's that?
Joe	A toothbrush.
Rita	It's white.
Roger	Is it your's Joe?
Joe	Yes.
Peter	How many have you got?
Suzy	Joe, I thought you said a black toothbrush — that's white.
Joe	I do have a black one — it's in my bag outside. I'll have to get

30

it when Pa. . . Paddy opens the door.

(Silence)

Peter	Then what are we all looking for?
Joe	I don't know.
Maureen	*(Laughs)* Well, it was fun anyway.
Peter	Holy Christ!
Suzy	Well okay, folks — that was an interesting, immediate exercise. Now let's just sit and talk before dinner.
Roger	Excellent idea. *(All sit)*
Suzy	So who wants to begin. Who wants to give a reaction to our new relationships . . .
Peter	I'd like to know why he goes on like that. Hiding. . . not talking. .
Suzy	Right. Do you feel that a barrier has been created?
Peter	I certainly do.
Suzy	Well, I'm sure Joe had his reasons for wanting to be alone, to be at peace with his thoughts. Right, Joe?
Joe	I didn't want to upset anyone anymore.
Roger	Oh, that's all in the past, Joe. We're all friends now. Rita and I have been very close — and Peter and Maureen too, of course. . .
Suzy	Right-on, Roger. So, just sit here with us Joe and talk. Open up. *(Silence)* Roger, you were telling me about your friend, remember? A lovely story — I'm sure that Joe, and the others, would like to share it.
Rita	I love stories — is it a nice story?
Roger	It's a sad, blue, soft story. It affected me deeply but I learned from it.
Suzy	We're all learning tonight — right, Maureen, Peter?
Peter	We are alright!
Maureen	Of course we are.
Suzy	Right, okay Roger — just as you told me.
Roger	Well, I was young, at boarding school and Tom was my chum, my best friend. . . .
Rita	That's nice. Tom — that's a nice name.
Roger	We shared everything. We sat together in class, we went for long walks in the afternoon, we roomed together . . . we. . . were close. It's hard to explain: you would have to have seen us together, to hear our laughter, to feel our silences, to know how much we depended upon each other, to really understand. I. . .I never thought that we could be anything but friends — until that summer when we parted for holidays.

31

	Tom was getting the train and I walked with him to the station and we said goodbye. I stood on the platform and he leaned from the carriage window and we stood there talking little things, farewell things. . .
Maureen	I know. *(To Peter)* When you went to Kerry to inspect the housing site — like that. Do you remember I went to the station. Do you remember. . . ?
Peter	*(Stiffly)* Of course I do.
Rita	My husband used to be like that too.
Roger	Well, something happened to the train that day — it was broken or the signals went wrong — anyway it didn't move. It just stayed there in the station and I stood on the platform and Tom was leaning out towards me and . . . then we were saying nothing. We didn't even look at each other, after a while. I was embarrassed — no, annoyed — at our silence, at our uncomfortable silence and I knew that he, like me, was just praying that the damn train would move. But it didn't. It just stayed there. It just stayed. . .
Suzy	You had said everything, right?
Roger	Yes, yes — but it was more than that. We both felt it. It wasn't that we had just said our goodbyes, it was as if. . . as if we had said everything. . . for ever. We were sudden strangers — and I could not even remember what had ever brought us close. I couldn't remember a single thing that we had in common. I couldn't even remember what we had lost.
Rita	My husband had a friend who was a doctor and *he* had a friend like that. But they had a lot in common. . . they were never strangers. . .
Roger	Well, Tom and I *were* strangers — from that moment. And when the train eventually moved, he just nodded and I turned away and ran down that platform. I didn't even wait to see if he waved — I'm sure he didn't — I'm sure he hated me in that instant.
Rita	I'm sure he didn't. . .
Roger	He never wrote — all through that summer, he never wrote and. . .and I knew that I would never see him again. I knew — and I knew why.
Maureen	I think you should have written, Roger.
Roger	No no, it would have been no good.
Maureen	A new relationship could have developed *(To Peter)* like when you were in Kerry and I wrote to you every day. Do you

	remember?
Pater	That was different, Maureen.
Maureen	Was it?
Peter	*(Softly)* We were married, for God's sake.
Roger	Nothing would ever have been the same again . . . People are like that — well, I believed for many years that they were and, in that time, I learned that only the animal — without deep feelings — can escape this. I believed that, for a long time. *(Silence)*
Suzy	So what did you do, Roger?
Roger	Well, I have tried. . .I have really tried to re-discover people . . . and myself. I have succeeded and I have failed. But sic itur ad astra — such is the way of the stars. My failure has been shown in my complete impersonal dedication to the arts: I am narcissian, you know — I am, I know I am. My success began when I started Group Therapy. And I have found that I'm not alone — that there were others. . .
Rita	I am miserable too.
Roger	Yes, and I'd like to relate to you, Rita. . .
Rita	Would you?
Roger	I really would. I really would.
Suzy	You see, we all seek happiness and understanding through communications and it is there for those who just open out, honestly. I'm sure you see that in this Session, Roger.
Maureen	I think that Joe is very lonesome. Are you Joe?
Joe	Me? No.
Maureen	I feel that you are.
Peter	If he says he's not, he's not. Get a grip on yourself.
Roger	I wonder, Peter. Did you ever lose, Joe? I mean, lose as I lost Tom. Did that ever happen to you?
Joe	*(Quietly)* I don't want to upset anyone anymore.
Suzy	Oh, you won't — we are all your family and we want to hear of your hopes, your plans, your dreams.
Joe	My dreams. . .?
Roger	Just tell us, Joe. We can help.
Joe	I had a cat once. . . when I was young.
Suzy	Good Joe, tell us about it.
Roger	*(To Rita)* You'll be interested in this, Rita — you like cats.
Rita	Was it a black cat, Joe — Judas was black, you know.
Joe	It was blue. I gave it milk every day and it was big and fat with thick glossy fur and black eyes and in the evening I would sit

	at the fire and it would cuddle at my feet and purr and stretch on its back and I would run my hand over its belly and. . . .
Rita	Joe? It couldn't have been a blue cat. There are no blue cats.
Joe	No, it was black — like my toothbrush. I remember.
Peter	Christ!
Rita	*(To Roger)* Like Judas. Judas was black with thick fur. . .
Maureen	What was your cat's name, Joe?
Joe	It was. . . it was Maureen. I called him Maureen. I loved her very much.
Maureen	*(Laughs)* Oh dearey me.
Peter	Wait a minute. Why did you have to call her Maureen?
Roger	No Peter, this could explain a lot. This is interesting.
Peter	What's interesting?
Roger	This is. This could be an association of names. I had that once with a . . . with a person I knew. Names haunt like smells, like music — they all become associations.
Suzy	Do you still have your cat, Joe?
Joe	No *(Pause)* No, when I was fifteen, I took her out, I carried her under my coat, along the road, up the hill to the railway bridge. I kept saying to her 'I love you, Maureen; I love you, Maureen; I love you Maureen . . . . '
Peter	Get on with your story, for God's sake — what happened?
Joe	Nothing happened.
Roger	You brought her home again?
Rita	We used to do that with our twelve cats — our apostles — take them out for a walk. Only we used to go in our car. My husband used to drive. He was a wonderful driver.
Suzy	Did you bring her home again Joe? *(Silence)*
Joe	I climbed the wall beside the bridge and carried her down the embankment to the railway line to wait for the train. We sat in the grass waiting for the train. She was purring, I was sleepy *(Pause)* and after the train passed, I carried her home again.
Roger	Why did you do that, Joe?
Joe	Because I loved her.
Peter	Loved her? She must have been terrified by the train, for God's sake.
Rita	Our cats were never terrified in the car. . .
Suzy	Did you often do that, Joe?
Joe	No, just once.
Roger	Ah, I see. . .

34

Joe	. . . I buried her in the garden beside the wall.
Maureen	Alive? You buried her alive?
Peter	Oh suffering Christ!
Joe	No No — she was dead.
Maureen	Ah, she died?
Rita	Did she die?
Joe	Yes, she died when I threw her under the train. . . .
Maureen	You threw her under the. . . ?
Joe	I just held her out as the train approached, let her see it, and she kicked and struggled and screamed. . .
Rita	*(Holding her chest)* Roger, I don't like this. . .
Roger	Quite. I really think we should. . .
Joe	. . . and as the noise came nearer, I could see the driver's face, looking at me, and I just held her out. . .
Peter	For Christ sake!
Joe	. . . and tossed her under the wheels. . .
Rita	No no — stop it. . . I don't want to hear. . .
Maureen	Joe, I don't really believe that you really. . .
Joe	. . . and Maureen screamed — just once — a long scream above the rattle of the wheels.
Peter	Shut up, shut up you mad bastard. *(Rises)*
Suzy	*(Rises)* Okay, okay that's enough. Settle down.
Rita	My heart! *(Searches her bag)* I don't feel well. . . my pills, my pills. . .
Roger	Are you alright? I'll get some water. *(Dashes to Contemplation Room)*
Joe	. . . and there was blood all along the line. . .
Peter	For Christ's sake — shut up!
Joe	. . . and the grass was speckled with blood. . .
Suzy	Enough! That's enough . . . that's enough!
Joe	*(Shouts)* And then I woke up! *(Silence. Roger dashes in with a glass of water)*
Maureen	You woke? It was all a dream? A nightmare?
Rita	A dream?
Roger	A dream? What was all a dream?
Peter	He says it was all a bloody dream. The whole thing.
Rita	A dream. It was a dream, wasn't it, Joe? *(Silence)*
Roger	The water, Rita.
Rita	No, I'm alright now. It was a dream.
Suzy	Joe, was that a dream?

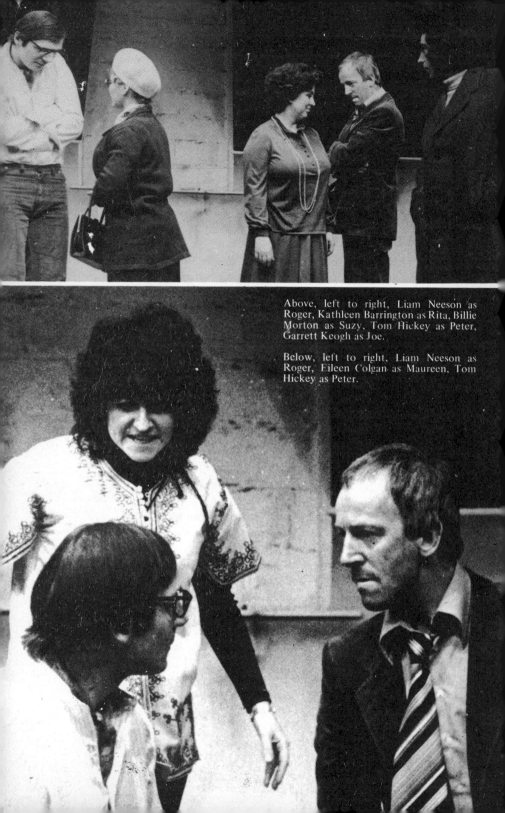

Above, left to right, Liam Neeson as Roger, Kathleen Barrington as Rita, Billie Morton as Suzy, Tom Hickey as Peter, Garrett Keogh as Joe.

Below, left to right, Liam Neeson as Roger, Eileen Colgan as Maureen, Tom Hickey as Peter.

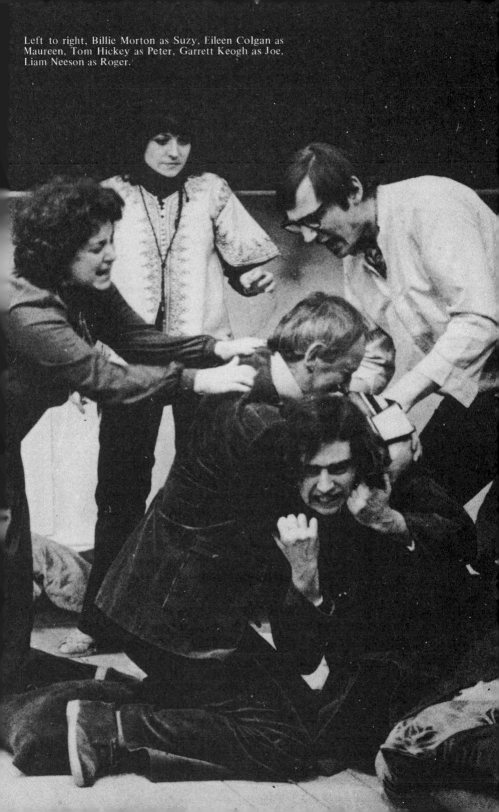
Left to right, Billie Morton as Suzy, Eileen Colgan as Maureen, Tom Hickey as Peter, Garrett Keogh as Joe, Liam Neeson as Roger.

Joe	Yes. When I woke, I was sitting on the embankment and a sparrow was singing and it was quiet and peaceful and I was looking up along the line and the sun was shining on the rails and this little ladybird jumped onto the back of my hand and I watched it and it was so peaceful. . . and warm. . .
Rita	And. . . where was. . . where was Maureen?
Peter	Maureen my arse!
Maureen	Peter, listen.
Suzy	Where was your cat, Joe?
Joe	With me. Purring. Years later she died — savaged by dogs — and I buried her in the garden. . .
Peter	For the love of God, do you know what you're talking about. . .
Joe	A dream. I'm sorry *(Stammer returns)* I. . . I'm sorry about your heart, Rita. . . I'm so. . . sorry if I upset you, Maureen. . . I'm sorry if you're ann. . . annoyed, Roger. . . Peter, I'm sorry. . .
Rita	It was a horrible story, Joe.
Roger	It most certainly was.
Joe	You asked me. . . you all asked me. You asked me for my dreams. . .
Suzy	Not those kind. . . okay, okay, settle down, folks.
Roger	Well, I must say that I found it very upsetting. However, we are a family —as Suzy says — and we shall try to help you, Joe.
Joe	Yes. I'm so sorry.
Suzy	That's okay, now, Joe.
Joe	It was a dream — but it was true. . . a true dream.
Roger	You should have said it was a dream — even if it *was* true.
Joe	It *was* true — as true as. . .as. . . as. . . As true as I'm an electrician.
Peter	But *are* you a bloody electrician?
Suzy	Now Peter, he said he was. . .
Peter	He said a lot of things *(To Joe)* What's the speed of light?
Joe	The what?
Peter	Speed! The speed of light! What is it? If you are an electrician you'll know that.
Suzy	Now Peter, hold it — we don't go checking out everyone. We rely on honesty.
Maureen	Yes, that's fair, Peter.
Peter	Fair? For Christ's sake, Maureen!
Joe	186,000 miles per second.

Suzy	There. Is that right, Peter?
Peter	I suppose so.
Joe	And the voltage multiplied by the amperage gives watts.
Maureen	*(Laughing)* What's watts?
Suzy	Yeah, what what. Okay great — we're all together again. The Session is going just great.
Rita	Was your cat really savaged by dogs?
Joe	Yes, she was.
Rita	That's terrible. Just like my husband. Do you take tablets?
Joe	Tablets?
Rita	For your nerves.
Maureen	I'm sure he doesn't.
Joe	I don't.
Rita	You should, really.
Peter	Bloody cyanide tablets!
Maureen	Peter!
	(Key is turned in door. Paddy enters with a tray)
Suzy	*(Springs to life)* Ah food! Hi, Paddy. Okay people time-out now for eats. Let's just relax, relate, communicate as we eat. We've passed the first Session — we've learned a lot and we're still learning from each other. The Therapy is really going great. . . really great. . .
Paddy	Will I put it inside?
Suzy	Yeah right, Paddy. Into the Contemplation Room.
Paddy	Very well, Miss *(Paddy smiles at Joe as he goes)*.
Joe	*(To all)* I'm really sorry.
Roger	It's perfectly all right now, Joe. I'm starving.
Suzy	Sure, sure Joe — come on, folks. Ah, you can get your black toothbrush now, Joe, if you wish. . .
Peter	*(To Maureen)* Come on, come on.
Maureen	*(Laughing)* I'm coming, I'm coming, I am coming!
Suzy	Paddy? Paddy? Paddy! *(Paddy runs out)* Paddy, Joe wants his bag for a moment, okay?
Paddy	Oh right, Miss — this way, sunshine.
	(As everyone leaves, Joe waits for Paddy to get the bag. Looks around room . Goes to phone box)
Paddy	*(With Joe's bag)* Here you are, sunshine — leaving already?
Joe	No, just get. . .get. . .getting a toothbrush.
Paddy	Thought you got that earlier.
Joe	*(Searching bag)* No, I forgot it.
Paddy	Fair enough — you work away there while I get the other

37

	trays. How's it going anyway — did Victoria get them off her yet? *(Carries tray through)*
Joe	*(Searching)* No, nothing li. . . like that.
Paddy	Glad to hear it — that'd put you off women for life. *(Passing by)* Find that toothbrush?
Joe	Yes, I got it. It was at the bottom. Will I leave the bag outside?
Paddy	*(With another tray)* Oh right. Just put it in the closet out-side. *(Joe leaves with bag)*
Roger	*(From room)* Who will say grace?
Maureen	*(From room)* I will — 'grace ' — there, I've said it. *(General laughter)*
Joe	*(Returning — meets Paddy from room)* I put it in the closet.
Paddy	Right sunshine — hey, tell us, was I right about them?
Joe	Well, they're not very hon. . . honest. We just had a se. . . session in which we were all supposed to. . .
Paddy	Don't tell me, sunshine — I've had enough troubles. Went home to find one of the chiselers fell off the shed. The whole side of his arm scraped. Lucky it wasn't broke. And the bleedin' telly is on the blink — and the wife's got one of her headaches. Jaysus, I'm telling you, if this goes on, I'll be in here myself next week.
Joe	Ah, you wouldn't fi. . .fi. . .fit in here.
Paddy	Jas, I don't know.
Joe	Did you find out about Texaleto?
Paddy	About what. . . ? . . .ah, Texale. .?. . .No, you didn't tell me. . .
Joe	Doesn't matter. When are you coming back?
Paddy	Back? Oh back at 7.00 am sharp to turn youse all loose, God help us. Better get going now *(Shouts)* I'm off now, Miss Bernstein.
Suzy	*(From room)* Okay Paddy, see you at 700 hours. Thanks a million. Come on, Joe — the food's getting cold.
Paddy	Not a bleedin' wave this time. Alright, sunshine — see you in the morning.
Joe	Yes, goodbye Paddy *(Waves to Paddy)* *(Paddy leaves. Door is locked. Joe waits. Goes to Telephone box again)*
Suzy	From room)* Joe! Joe are you coming? We're eating here like bears. *(Laughter)*
Maureen	*(From room)* Come on, Joe — I've kept a dough-nut for you *(More laughter)*

Joe	Alright, I'm coming. . .
	(Joe quickly reaches out, holds the phone flex and pulls it from the wall. Conceals the loose part in the socket. Glances around the room)
Suzy	Joe! Joe, what's keeping you?
Joe	I'm coming *(Goes to room)* Here I am *(Closes door)*

End of Act One

Curtain

ACT TWO
SCENE ONE

(Suzy, Roger, Rita and Maureen are sitting, talking. Peter and Joe are off-stage in the Contemplation Room)

Maureen	*(Laughing)* Come on, Rita — you're not trying.
Rita	I am I am — I can *see* my twelve little pussy-cats — it's putting names on them that is difficult. Now — Peter, Andrew, James, John, Philip. . . Bartholomew. . .oh, dear. . . Philip. . . Bartholomew. . . Bartholomew
Roger	Ah Rita, you have forgotten . Yet, at spes non fracta. . .
Rita	No no — I haven't forgotten — I'm just trying to picture them: I see Bartholomew now, a big lad Bartholomew, proud — now, who's that behind you, Bartholomew? Ah, Thomas. How could I forget little Thomas.
Maureen	That's eight. Come on — four to go.
Rita	Four to go. Thomas . . . Thomas. . .
Roger	You said to him, Rita.
Rita	Yes, I know. John, Philip, Bartholomew, Thomas. . . Matthew?
Suzy	Matthew. Right. Three more.
Peter	*(Shouts from room)* Well, what the hell's that got to do with you?
Rita	Bartholomew, Thomas, Matthew . . .
Maureen	*(Looking towards room)* Peter?
Rita	No, I said Peter.
Maureen	Peter, is something the matter? Joe?
Suzy	It's okay, Maureen — they're just sorting something out, I guess. Let them be.
Maureen	They've been in there for ages.
Roger	It's good to see Joe opening-up. He was very quiet at the start.
Suzy	Joe is an introvert — needs a lot of sympathy.
Peter	*(From room)* I said No — that's final No!
Rita	Thomas. . . and Matthew. . .
Roger	Pity we're missing it, really — I'd honestly like to know what's so important in there.

40

Rita	It's James.
Maureen	Who is James?
Rita	He's the striped one.
Maureen	Oh, the cats.
Peter	*(Shouts)* Rubbish! Absolute rubbish!
Rita	. . . and Thaddius. . . James, Thaddeus . . .
Peter	*(Shouts)* No, we won't ask her — we bloody well won't.
Suzy	Hi, you two — is that a private exchange or will you come out and let the family join in?
Maureen	I'm going to see *(Runs to Contemplation Room)*
Rita	How many is that, Roger?
Roger	Oh, I don't know, Rita. . . I'm sorry, I haven't been counting. Suzy, how many was that?
Suzy	Was it eleven?
Roger	Yes, that's right. Eleven. One to go.
Rita	One to go. Let me see now. My husband, you know, could name them like a song. Where is pussy number twelve? Simon! Simon, you bad cat — hiding from my memory.
Roger	Bravo Rita — that's the famous twelve.
Maureen	*(From room)* Tell me, Peter, tell me. . .
Peter	No, no, no, it is nothing. This. . . this. . . mad bastard. . . sorry love. . . come on, we're going out. . . *(Maureen appears)*
Maureen	*(Looking back)* I'd like to know what he said.
Peter	*(Appearing)* It was nothing. . . a load of shhh. . . load of rubbish.
Roger	Hello there.
Suzy	Hi people, can the family help?
Roger	We sit in the hope of being asked.
Peter	*(Sitting)* It's private.
Roger	It shouldn't be. Not to the family — not within the circle.
Peter	Well it bloody-well is.
Maureen	Peter! Don't talk like that, please.
Peter	I bloody-well will talk like that.
Rita	Judas!
Peter	What the hell do you mean by that?
Rita	Judas — he's another. I forgot Judas.
Suzy	Rita has been naming her twelve cats for us.
Peter	Oh, for Christ's sake — not again.
Maureen	Peter! What has annoyed you so much?
Peter	It's not me — it's that fool out there with his lies and . . .

41

	his games and . . . his bloody insinuations.
Roger	Tell us. Peter — we can help, we really can. Our arms are open, our minds are awakened, we sit in hope to hear you verbatim et litteratim . . .
Peter	Will you cut that out — that fancy, educated talk. He's no right to say . . . what he said.
Maureen	What did he say?
Peter	Never mind!
Suzy	*(Controlled)* Peter, when we're strung-up, up-tight, we cannot communicate and our problems just grow and grow out of all proportion. So, unless you really feel that we shouldn't know, why not just unwind and tell us your problem.
Peter	It's not *my* problem — it's his. *(Indicates room)*
Joe	*(Appearing)* Hello family.
Roger	Ah, welcome Joe.
Peter	Don't sit near me — I'm warning you.
Maureen	Peter!
Peter	And don't sit near her. *(Indicates Maureen)*
Maureen	Oh, for Heaven's sake.
Peter	Yes, for Heaven's sake.
Suzy	Sit here, Joe — beside Rita. Okay Rita?
Rita	That's thirteen apostles — thirteen cats, Judas makes thirteen. Did I count them properly, Roger? Oh sorry, Suzy — what did you say?
Suzy	Joe is going to sit here beside you — that okay?
Rita	Oh yes, do sit here, Joe. Can you name the twelve apostles?
Joe	Yes.
Rita	Can you really?
Joe	*(Quietly)* Yes. Peter, Andrew, James, John, Philip, Bartholomew, Thomas, James and Thaddeus, Matthew, Simon and Judas.
Suzy	That is fantastic, Joe.
Roger	Yes indeed — mirabile, mirabile. Congratulations.
Joe	Thanks *(Pause)* And there's no record of any of them having any children.
Peter	*(Jumping up)* Christ! I'll kill you if you don't shut your. . .
Maureen	Peter, sit down. He didn't say anything.
Peter	I know what he's saying — and I'm not going to sit here and listen. . .
Suzy	Easy now, easy. Don't get up-tight. Keep it cool. Now what's the problem? *(Peter sits)* Come on.
Peter	Change the subject.

42

Suzy	Joe, what's this all about? Tell the family. What did you say?
Joe	Me? I just said that they had no children.
Peter	Leave it at that now — everyone knows we have no children. We decided not to. . .
Joe	I said the apostles had no children — not you. *(Silence)*
Maureen	Was that it, Peter? Was it? About us having no children?
Peter	Part of it. . .
Suzy	Ah Peter, that's fine. Take it easy. We know all about that — we've had that. That's okay.
Peter	You know too much — all of you. And it's all his bloody fault. . .
Joe	Me?
Roger	Look, Peter, you're hyper-sensitive about this — and I can understand. It's very common — people become hyper-sensitive about things that other people don't even notice.
Suzy	That is so true, you know.
Roger	I had a friend — a charming person — who had a mole on his. . . her leg and, do you know, she never went out swimming. She would never take off her clothes in public — never! He thought that nobody ever saw anything *except* the mole — but nobody ever noticed her damn mole. *(Pause)* Look, talking of children, Rita had none — but she's not sensitive about it. Are you Rita?
Rita	I had twelve — but I've counted thirteen now.
Peter	Holy Christ!
Roger	No — children, Rita, not cats.
Rita	Oh no, we didn't have any children. . . I would have liked a daughter like Suzy or Maureen. . . or a son like you, Roger. . or Peter. . .
Joe	Or me?
Rita	Of course, Joe — or you.
Peter	A fine son he'd make!
Rita	Yes, a fine son. . . or Roger or a daughter like Maureen or Suzy or. . .
Maureen	Now Peter — it's alright, isn't it?
Peter	Is it?
Roger	But what else is the problem? *(To Maureen)* I mean you *can* have children if you want them. . . can't you?
Maureen	Of course he can, if he would just learn to relax and to. . .
Peter	Maureen! Will you shut up! Do you know what you're saying?

	Listen to the bloody question — he asked about *you* not me.
Maureen	But Peter, *I* can. . .
Roger	You can. You mean that Peter. . .
Peter	Alright! Terrific! Let the whole, curious, interfering family in on it. *You* can. Great — you never stop trying, do you? Did you all hear that. Maureen can have children. I can't. The cat's out of the bag.
Rita	The cat?
Peter	Yes, the bloody cat — all your bloody cats. Why didn't *you* have children. Let's all be honest. What was wrong with you . . . or your husband?
Roger	Now just a moment, Peter — there's absolutely no need. . .
Peter	You! We all know why you can't. I'm asking her. *(To Rita)* Well, why didn't you have children?
Rita	I don't see why you have to shout at me.
Peter	I'll ask you quietly then: why didn't you have children? Tell the family. We are all ready to help. We're all just dying to help. Tell us. . .
Suzy	I don't think, Peter, we ought to. . .
Rita	*(Softly)* I'm not well, Roger. Will you get me some water?
Roger	*(Jumping up)* Yes, of course, Rita. . .
Maureen	*(Jumping up)* I need some too — after that mad outburst. Peter, you really ought to . . .
Peter	Why are you leaving all of a sudden? Are you after him now? He's not going to be much use to you, you know. What's going to happen out there? And after him, who will it be? One of the twelve cats?
Maureen	Peter! Peter, you promised not to mention that sort of thing.
Rita	Joe, will you pass my handbag, please — my tablets. . .
Roger	*(Who has paused)* I'll get the water.
Maureen	No, you sit down, Roger — I'll get enough for all of us. . .
Peter	Bloody Gunga Din now. First, Jezebel the man chaser; now Gunga Din the water carrier. . .
Maureen	Stop it, Peter.
Peter	You want me to stop now — convenient — just when we come to your *little* problem.
Maureen	I'm getting the water. . .*(Leaves)*
Joe	Will I get out your tablets, Rita?
Rita	Thank you, Joe — you're a good boy. Where's the water?
Roger	Maureen is getting it.
	(Silence as Maureen returns with the water. Rita takes a tablet)

44

Suzy	Okay people, settle down — we've got nothing to worry about. We've had some reaction to our unmaskings and this is good. The Session is going well — very well. Now we can try to calmly and helpfully, sort it all out. You okay, Rita?
Rita	Yes, thank you. I don't like people shouting at me. I get turns, you know.
Suzy	Right. Peter, do you want to say something at this point in time?
	(Silence as Peter sulks)
Suzy	Roger?
Roger	Yes, well I think that we, inadvertently, did a disservice to Peter.
Joe	I agree.
Peter	Christ!
Suzy	Yes we did, Roger, That's so true.
Roger	We touched on a sensitive nerve — but not in the right way. Peter felt exposed, felt alienated and beyond our understanding. And he reacted. In Oslo, we often discovered that with a little help, this alienation can be. . .
Rita	If it will help, I'll answer Peter's question.
Suzy	Fine Rita — that's a positive and mature reaction to a here-and-now situation. Are you with us, Peter? *(Silence)* Okay, go ahead, Rita.
Rita	When we married, I thought of how many children we would have. Two boys, I thought, and one girl — the boys just like their father: quiet, sensitive and understanding — the girl, smiling and shy. We talked about it many times. I remember on our honeymoon — we took a cruise from Southampton to Malta — we would stand at the ship's rail, watching the surf, and talk of our dreams. My husband loved children and it was a great blow to us to realise that we could never have any. But we learned to accept this and it brought us even closer together. We never had our two boys, or our girl, but we had each other.
Maureen	*(Gently)* How long is your husband dead, Rita?
Rita	My husband died three years ago — savaged by dogs. That beautiful, gentle, quiet man who had so much to give to the world was savaged by dogs. I miss him so much.
Roger	Did you ever form — or try to form — another relationship after he . . . .died?
Rita	That would have been impossible, Roger. We didn't have our

	children but that didn't matter. Nobody — no man could ever have replaced him.
Peter	Not all wives are so devoted.
Maureen	*(Gently)* Don't say that, Peter.
Peter	Why not? It's true, isn't it. It's honest. . .
Maureen	Peter, I know what you're thinking and you know that it's not true.
Peter	Isn't it? Then what about Marcus Dalton or Tony what's-his-name or. . .
Maureen	Peter, don't.
Peter	Tell them about Marcus Dalton, Maureen. Tell them about the famous drive in his new car and the meals you had with him and your see-through dress and your hair all done up for him and. . .and. . .and the magazine he gave you with all the instructions. . .
Maureen	Peter please, you're only. . .
Peter	He did give you that magazine, didn't he? Was that how were both going to do it? Was it?
Maureen	Peter!
Rita	We never had any children, but we were so close. . .
Maureen	You've explained all that, Rita. He just won't see reason.
Peter	What reason?
Maureen	*(Quietly to all)* This Marcus Dalton was his business partner — architect — who one day took me for a drive in his new B.M.W. . .
Peter	All his great talk and his education and the dinners he had. . .
Maureen	. . . And Peter simply refused to come along. . .
Peter	. . . Come along! Ha! Did you want me to sit there and watch the two of you?
Maureen	You don't believe that Peter. Not really. . .
Peter	But I do! I do believe it!
Maureen	You know that there was nothing between Marcus Dalton and I. Nor anyone else. You know that — I've told you. . .
Peter	Can you swear to it? In front of everyone? Can you?
Roger	Oh Peter — really now. . .
Peter	Well can you? Ah. Can you?
Maureen	Yes!
Peter	Right. Go on, swear to it. Let me hear you — in front of everyone. . .
Suzy	Look Peter, I wonder if we could discuss this. . .
Peter	Discuss nothing — let me hear her swear. *(Silence)* See? What did I say? Now you have the two sides. Now you understand.

Maureen	I swear it! I swear that there was nothing between Marcus Dalton — or anyone else — and I. I swear it. Now.
Rita	That is lovely. Just like the marriage vows of my dear husband. . .
Suzy	Peter? Do you want to say something?
Roger	I think you honestly ought to acknowledge. . .
Suzy	It's vital for the Session that we. . .
Peter	*(Quietly)* Maureen. Do you really swear to that?
Maureen	Yes Peter, of course. Why did you have to do this?
Peter	It . . . it was because of. . .of what they said to me. . . the children and. . .
Maureen	You heard how Rita and her husband felt. I feel the same. I told you that.
Peter	Yes, it was what they said. . . I'm sorry. . . I. .
Suzy	Well, that's sorted out. Everything's AOK.
Maureen	*(To Peter)* Look love, why don't we go to the room for a while and. . . talk. . .
Peter	No no, we can't just go and. . .
Maureen	Come on now, come on. . .
Peter	I don't think we're supposed to leave. . .
Suzy	Sure you are, Peter. This is our world — this is the only here-and-now. You can do as you please.
Maureen	Now, come on, love. . .
Peter	*(Rising)* I don't think we ought to in front. . .
Maureen	Come on. Don't worry.
Suzy	Go ahead people. Fine *(Peter and Maureen leave)*
Rita	*(Sobbing)* I'm sorry. It reminds me of how my husband used to. . .
Suzy	That's okay, Rita — it's a great emotional release for all of us.
Roger	Amantium irae amoris integratio est.
Rita	Pardon?
Roger	Ah 'lovers quarrels are the renewal of love' — a quotation by Terence of Rome.
Joe	Homer of Greece.
Roger	Homer? No Terence, the Roman dramatist. Died 150 BC.
Joe	Homer, the Greek poet. Died 850 BC.
Roger	No, you're mistaken, Joe.
Joe	Yes, I'm not, Roger.
Suzy	Hey, what the hell, boys — we've all seen a deep-rooted problem solved through our understanding. Doesn't that make us all feel good. And Rita, your honesty made it all possible.

47

	Do you know that?
Rita	Do you think so?
Suzy	Sure, Rita.
Roger	It's true, Rita — you did.
Rita	Oh, do you really think so? Let's celebrate. *(Takes paper bag from her handbag)* Let's have sweets. Here Joe, have a Liquorice Allsort.
Joe	Oh thank you.
Rita	Suzy, have a sugary one. They're nice.
Suzy	Well, I shouldn't — but why the hell not.
Roger	Yes, be a devil. *(Also takes one)* Thank you Rita.
Rita	Take two, if you wish, Roger
Roger	No no, sufficient for the day and all that.
Rita	I'll have a three-tier one. Oh, I wish my husband were here now.
Suzy	He's here, Rita. In your heart, he's here.
Rita	Yes, perhaps he is.
Suzy	He is, Rita — he's here.
Roger	Yes, he is.
	(Silence)
Joe	Rita, did it take the ship long to get to Malta in those days?
Rita	Malta? Sorry Joe, what did you say?
Suzy	Joe was wondering how long it took your honeymoon ship to get to Malta.
Rita	Oh, the ship. Well now, Joe, that was a long time ago. I don't really remember. My memory is not good, you know.
Roger	Of course, we understand.
Rita	But it was a long voyage, I remember that. . . A long, beautiful voyage. *(Pause)* Sitting on the deck during the day, holding my husband's hand. And he in his whites — he looked so splendid. I remember how tall he was — he was tall and elegant. And the boy who brought us drinks — yes, I remember him. A young, Italian lad — he would always bow and call me 'your lady'. He was a lovely boy — he'd say 'Would your lady like some tea now' or 'Is your lady comfortable'. My husband used to be so proud. He was never jealous. Never.
Suzy	You remember quite a lot, Rita. Hey, bet you can even remember the name of the ship.
Rita	The name? Oh the name . . . yes. . eh, no. I'm afraid I can't. Perhaps. . .oh. . . . my husband could remember. He had a wonderful memory.

48

Suzy	I'm sure he had.
Roger	May I be permitted . . . may I. . . I would like to give a here-and-now reaction to Rita's recollection.
Rita	A what?
Roger	A family reaction. We used to do this in Oslo.
Suzy	Oh sure, Roger. A here-and-now reaction, family.
Roger	Well, I find it interesting that Rita, in recapturing these beautiful moments, has never mentioned her husband's name. And I wonder does anyone feel that there is, perhaps, a subconscious desire in this to preserve an intimate memory?
Rita	Oh no. . . did I say? . . .didn't I tell you. . .?
Suzy	Sure you did. You said his name was. . . Andrew?
Rita	Yes, that is. . . that was. . . I. . .
Roger	No surely, wasn't Andrew one of the names we were trying to remember for your cats?
Suzy	Right on, Roger. That is correct. So many names. . .
Rita	*(Upset)* Yes, Andrew. . . no, my husband's name was. . . Tom. Tom was his name. A nice name. Tom.
Roger	That is unbelievable, Rita.
Rita	Unbelievable? Why do you. . .?. . . it is *not* unbelievable. . .
Roger	No — that was just my friend's name at school. Do you remember? I told you about him. Tom.
Suzy	It was indeed.Tom.
Rita	Yes, Tom was my husband's name. Yes, I remember thinking of my husband when you spoke of your friend. *(Laughter from room)*
Suzy	Hey listen — really making it up in there now.
Rita	Yes, Tom was his name. Tom. He loved Malta.
Roger	It wasn't called Malta then, of course. Or was it?
Suzy	Sure it was. It was always called Malta.
Roger	Even before the war?
Suzy	Sure. Wasn't it, Rita?
Rita	Wasn't it what? I'm sorry. . .
Roger	Malta. It wasn't called Malta when you were there, was it?
Rita	Oh no. . . it was. .
Suzy	/ can't think of what it was called. . .
Rita	Would you like another sweet? A two-tier one?
Suzy	Not for me, Rita.
Roger	No, thank you, Rita.
Joe	Thank you *(Takes one)*
Roger	Ah, it was Persia I was thinking of.

Suzy	Persia?
Roger	That became Iran. Yes, Valetta is Malta's capital — Valetta, Rita?
Rita	*(Weakly)* We had a Persian cat, you know. That was Andrew. I remember now.
Suzy	*(Laughing)* How could you confuse Malta with Persia, Roger?
Roger	Oh, white heat perhaps. Sunshine. I don't know. I'd like to see Malta. Is it nice, Rita?
	(More laughter from room)
Rita	*(Fingering her ring)* It's nice to hear that. Do you like laughter, Suzy?
Suzy	Yeah, like music, I always say.
Roger	Malta is nice, then, yes?
Rita	Yes, my husband could always remember. He was always travelling . . .always going away. . . going away. . .
Suzy	*(Pause)* I've noticed your rings, Rita. They're beautiful.
Rita	*(Relieved)* Oh yes — this one was given to me by my brother. It's Sapphire.
Suzy	Ah, you're a Virgo?
Rita	No no . . . yes. . I. . . what did you say?
Suzy	Virgo — your birthstone. August/September.
Rita	Oh yes. I was born in August.
Suzy	Then you're a Virgo.
Rita	Oh, I see.
Suzy	And this is your wedding ring?
Rita	Oh yes. My husband put this on my finger *(Pulls ring from finger)* when we . . . would you like to see it?
Suzy	Sure — but I guess it's been so long on your finger that you cannot remove it now, can you?
Rita	*(Puts ring back)* No no, I can't — it's been so long. . .
Joe	*(Stammering again)* May I gi. . . give a here-and-now re. . . reaction. . . ?
Suzy	Sorry Joe?
Roger	Joe is quickly learning the modus operandi of our Group. He has a here-and-now reaction for us.
Suzy	Oh great. Sure Joe. What is it?
Joe	I th. .think from your questions that you do not believe that Rita was ever in Malta. . .
Rita	But I was. *(Upset)* I was. After we married, my husband took me. . .
Roger	Yes, of course. Joe I think you are greatly. . .

50

Joe	. . .and that you do. . .don't really believe that she was even ma. . .married. . . married.
Rita	I was, I was. . . I cannot remember because it was so long, but I was. . .
Suzy	Easy Rita, easy. That's just Joe's here-and-now.
Rita	Just because I cannot remember doesn't mean. . . he was always travelling. . . but he came back. . .he. . .
Roger	Of course, of course.
Rita	He promised to take me to Malta and he. . did. .
Suzy	Sure Rita, take it easy. . .
Roger	*(To Joe)* Look what you've done now!
Joe	I just have a here-and-now reaction to your questions. . .
Roger	For Heaven's sake, our questions were just communication. . .
Suzy	. . . conversation. . .
Joe	Inquisition!
Roger	What? No no, communication. Rita said she was married and we. . .
Rita	I was married to Tom . I told the truth. I was, I. . .*(Laughter from room)* . . .said I was. . . my husband was. . . *(More laughter)*. . . Who is laughing? Why are they laughing?
Suzy	Relax Rita, that's just Peter and Maureen. . .
Roger	It's perfectly all right now. . .
Rita	Well, I don't know. . .I can't remember. . . Can I have a glass of water. . . I take turns when I'm upset, you know. . .
Suzy	Fine. Roger, get some water, will you?
Roger	No, I'll get it, blast you.
Joe	*(Runs to Contemplation Room Door)* I'm getting it.
Suzy	Now Rita, you're fine. . .
Joe	*(Knocking at door)* Open up.
Maureen	*(From inside)* What is it, Joe?
Joe	I want a glass of water.
Peter	*(From inside)* For God's sake!
Roger	You're perfectly all right now, Rita.
Joe	*(Door is opened. Joe enters)* Just want water. *(Door is closed)*
Rita	Can I have a glass of water?
Suzy	Joe is getting it, okay?
Rita	I was married . . . I was..
Suzy	Of course Rita — do you have a tablet? *(Joe returns with water)* Ah here's the water.
Roger	*(To Joe)* Give it to me.
Joe	No, I'll do it.

51

Roger	Give it to me *(Takes glass)* Now Rita, sip this slowly.
Suzy	There. Do you have a tablet?
Joe	She has them in her bag. . .
Rita	No, I'll rest now. I just want to rest. Just to rest.
Roger	Yes, do *(Stands. To Joe)* You and your talk. What an idiot thing to do!
Joe	It was just a here-and-no. . . now. . .
Roger	You didn't have to say it.
Joe	You. . .you. . .you were saying it.
Roger	I certainly was not.
Joe	I was only being ho. . . honest in a here-and-now . . .
Suzy	*(Standing. They move away from Rita)* Okay, drop it. She's resting now. She's fine.
Maureen	*(From room)* Peter — No! *(Laughter)*
Peter	Yabadaba-dooooooooo. *(Laughter)*
Roger	There was absolutely no need for this to happen.
Joe	You me . . . mean she could have told us?
Roger	Told us what?
Joe	That she wasn't marr . . . married.
Roger	Who said she wasn't, for Heaven's sake?
Suzy	Okay, okay, leave it at that — we've got another problem now.
Roger	What other problem?
Suzy	*(Sternly)* I'll give it to you straight. Peter and Maureen's re-conciliation is based on Rita's story — right?
Roger	That's true yes.
Suzy	Now I don't want this new experience to be spoiled — I don't want this whole Session ruined by someone deciding to blow this whole thing about Rita wide open. I want no reference to it whatsoever.
Roger	Look Suzy, do you think it would be better if we just said there was a misunderstanding . . . ?
Suzy	*(Mock good humour)* Roger, just relax . . .
Joe	. . . . relate, communicate . . . .
Suzy	*(Angrily)* Shut up, Joe! *(Sternly to Roger)* What I want done, I want done for the sake of the Session. This Session is going to work and I'm not going to have . . . .
Joe	Sh . . . Sh . . shouldn't we be honest?
Roger	Well, that's rich coming from you, I must say.
Suzy	Drop it please! I'm going to ask for a show of hands right now. Do we skip what was said about Rita? *(Movements heard from Contemplation Room)*
Maureen	*(From room)* Peter, come on . . . come on . . .

Peter	*(From room)* Yabadaba-doooooooo.
Maureen	Peter! *(Laughter)* That's enough — we're going out now. *(Laughter)*
Suzy	Look, we've got to decide now — we can't upset the whole Session by . . .
Joe	Do . . do . . does Rita have a vote?
Suzy	*(Angrily)* Right! If I don't get an immediate show of hands, I'm phoning Paddy. *(Joe shoots up his hand)* That's one. Roger, I want it unanimous.
Roger	*(Slowly)* I'm not so sure, but . . . *(he raises his hand)* Oh well . . . .
Suzy	*(Now more relaxed)* Okay folks, we can all hang loose now. *(They return to their places)* Everything's going to be okay — I'll make this Session work. Just relax . . . .
Joe	. . . relate, communicate. Relax, relate, communicate . . .
Roger	Do you have to act the parrot at a time like this? *(Peter and Maureen enter. They are holding hands)*
Suzy	Hey, you're looking good, people.
Maureen	We are good — aren't we, love?
Peter	Oh, we're good alright. I'm good, you're good, we're good. Yabadaba-dooooooooo.
Maureen	Oh dear, poor Rita — is she alright?
Joe	She took a turn.
Suzy	No, she didn't. She's fine. She's resting. We had a long conversation. Didn't we, Roger?
Roger	Yes, we had indeed.
Maureen	Poor dear — it is late, of course. We wanted her to tell us more about her husband and Malta, didn't we, Peter?
Peter	That's true, love — we did.
Suzy	Well, she's sleeping now — hey, did you two talk it all out?
Maureen	Oh, we talked alright . . . .
Peter	. . . occasionally and a bit of yabadaba-doooooo.
Maureen	*(Lightly)* Please Peter — yes, we had a great talk — our first real discusssion for years — taiked about our lives and *(to Peter)* dare I mention, Marcus Dalton?
Peter	You may dare — just once.
Suzy	That's really good. So you've sorted it out, eh?
Maureen	We have. And we owe it all to Rita — and to you all, of course.
Roger	Yes, we understand.
Peter	If she hadn't told us about her life, we would . . .
Suzy	Great. See, the Group is working, working . . . and while

	you were out, we were solving problems, making decisions, becoming aware . . .
Joe	. . . taking votes . . .
Roger	Joe! We were just talking . . .
Maureen	Oh, you must tell us what you discussed . . . .
Rita	*(Awake)* I miss him so much . . . Tom. I miss Tom . . . .
Roger	That's alright, Rita.
Peter	Ah, she's awake.
Maureen	Rita? Hello — we wanted to ask you . . .
Rita	*(Sipping water)* I had a sleep . . . .
Suzy	Okay, we'll leave that for a while — eh, would anyone like to discuss anything else . . .? Like to discuss anything? Anything? Roger?
Joe	I want to talk about something.
Roger	Now Joe, don't forget . . . what we said.
Peter	You said? What was said?
Suzy	Okay, okay, fine. Right Joe, what do you want to talk about?
Maureen	Something happy?
Joe	*(Happily)* Yes, a funny story.
Suzy	Great, Joe — go ahead.
Joe	Not about Malta.
Roger	For Heaven's sake, Joe . . .
Joe	I said *not* about Malta. It's funny.
Roger	Your ideas of fun are . . .
Rita	I like funny stories. I like laughter.
Suzy	Like music — eh Rita?
Rita	Yes, I like music *(Searches her handbag)*.
Joe	It's about my father . . .
Maureen	Oh lovely. Come on, Joe — you never mentioned your father before.
Joe	Well, when I was young, my father . . .
Rita	*(Still searching handbag)* Wait, I've got to see if my tablets are . . . oh, here they are.
Suzy	You okay, Rita?
Rita	Yes. I just like to know where they are.
Joe	Well, when I was young, my father was a porter in a railway station and he had a little cap and a worsted uniform and he used to tear tickets in half — or clip them — and wave a green flag . . .
Roger	We know what porters do!
Maureen	Shhhhhhh.

54

Joe	And he had a little silver whistle with a pea in it and he used to blow it when the train was ready to leave . . .
Roger	*(Quietly, anxiously to Suzy)* Is this about his train again?
Joe	It's a *funny* story.
Suzy	Go ahead, Joe — it's okay, Roger.
Joe	Anyway, one day — it was summer — the train had to take on five churns of milk and my father was helping the guard of the train with the churns, when they suddenly noticed this boy standing on the platform saying goodbye to an older boy who was on the train. So, for a laugh — my father could be very funny — they decided to be as slow as they could — so that they would leave the two boys talking. So they kept rolling the five churns onto the train and taking them off again and the boys were still there — and then my father said that he'd like to check the wheels on the train — and that took more time — and then they took the five churns off again — and then, suddenly, a police car stopped outside the station and these two policemen got out — and there was a tall, greyhaired man with them. And my father knew that man — he was the headmaster of the local boarding school. And the policemen and the man ran along the platform and grabbed the boy who was saying goodbye and took him away . . .
Peter	Hey, that sounds very like Roger's story of saying goodbye to his . . . his . . . his friend.
Maureen	To Tom, you mean.
Joe	No, no, it's different — Roger didn' say anything about the police . . .
Rita	And what happened, Joe?
Joe	Well the boy on the train was shouting and screaming at them. So my father blew the whistle with the little pea in it, waved his green flag and the train went off. *(Silence)*
Maureen	Is that all?
Joe	Yes.
Maureen	But why was he screaming?
Joe	What?
Peter	Why did the police come?
Joe	Oh. Well, my father knew the headmaster and he said that they were taking the boy back to school to finish his studies.
Peter	Oh.
Joe	Yes, my father heard later that he became a priest and went on the missions to the Philippines.

Maureen	And what about the other boy?
Joe	Ah. He was expelled from the school — but the funny part of the story was my father putting the churns on the train and taking them off again. *(Silence)*
Peter	*(Weakly)* Yes, that's funny alright.
Suzy	Right, Fine. Eh, you liked your father, Joe?
Joe	I used to see him at the station — blowing his whistle and waving his flag.
Suzy	But you liked him?
Joe	The boy's name was Roger, I think.
Rita	Roger? That's the same as . . . *(indicates Roger)*
Suzy	Which boy? The one who became a padre?
Joe	A priest. No, I don't know what his name was.
Suzy	The other one?
Joe	He was . . . .
Rita	Roger? Why, that's a coincidence. My husband's name was Tom, and Tom's friend was Roger, and Roger is the name of . . .
Joe	*(Quietly)* I heard that he was expelled from school because, one night, there was a younger boy who . . .
Roger	That's it! I knew it! I've been waiting for this . . . this is another of this fool's lies, his insinuations . . . I know what you're saying.
Suzy	Roger!
Roger	He's an incurable liar, that bastard. He's . . .
Rita	Roger, you're shouting.
Suzy	Hold it, Roger.
Maureen	What is this all about?
Joe	I don't know — I just heard my father saying that . . .
Roger	Don't you know? It's about me, isn't it? I'm supposed to be . . .
Suzy	Roger, calm down. Let the family analyse this . . .
Roger	Don't analyse me with those lies.
Joe	You're hypersensitive, Roger.
Rita	Why is everybody shouting?
Roger	Hypersensitive!
Joe	Yes, like what Peter said about the boy he knew with the mole on his leg who would never take off his trousers when he went swimming . . .
Maureen	*(Laughing)* What boy, Peter? I didn't know you knew a boy with a mole on his leg . . .

Peter	I don't know any boy! Get a grip on yourself!
Roger	That was me, for Heaven's sake.
Rita	Do you have a mole on your leg, Roger?
Suzy	No, it's Roger's story, Rita. You remember: nobody noticed the boy's mole, but *he* was so sensitive about it.
Joe	Roger is hypersensitive — like that boy.
Roger	Hypersensitive be damned! It's this bastard who . . .
Joe	No no no — why is everyone getting *(Stammering again)* ex . . . ex . . excited? It was a fu . . . funny story . . .
Roger	And that's another one of your tricks — that stammer . . .
Maureen	Now Roger, that's not fair.
Suzy	Yes, I don't think it's right to . . .
Roger	It's all games, lies, tricks . . .
Joe	Not lies . . my father told me that the train . . .
Roger	Was that like the train you threw your cat under?
Rita	His cat? What cat?
Maureen	*(Laughing)* Look, I really think we ought to . . .
Roger	Yes cats. You upset everyone with that and then you tried to make Rita say that she didn't marry her husband and go to Malta . .
Peter	What? Didn't she say . . ?
Roger	. . . well, you're not going to make me admit . . .
Peter	But didn't she go to Malta? You told us that . . . Rita, you told Maureen and I that . . . .
Roger	To hell with Maureen and you! He did the same to you and were it not for Rita, your marriage would be in bits.
Peter	Our marriage is not in bits!
Roger	And if you now believe that his father ever worked on the trains . . . .
Joe	He ne . . never worked on the trains . . .
Roger	Ah see? The story is changed again. So he never worked on the trains . . .
Joe	He was a porter in the station. I said that.
Roger	Just listen to him.
Joe	I merely said that my fa. . . father told me that Roger was expelled from school . .
Roger	*(Shouting at Joe)* Shut up! Don't start that again.
Suzy	Okay okay okay. That's enough, folks.
Rita	I don't like all this shouting . . . my husband never shouted . . . he was gentle . . .
Suzy	Yeah okay. Now everything is fine. Let's get it all sorted out.

	We've had an exchange — now lets pause, hang loose and re-lax. Let's think of the Session, okay? Okay Joe — you have said that . . .
Roger	Yes, let's have some more lies . . .
Suzy	Roger, there's probably a good explanation . . .
Roger	Oh there is — he's a liar, that's the explanation. He has an eternal string of lies . . . come on, then let's have some more. Come on . . .
Joe	I do . . . don't think that anyone was really being hon . . . honest about . . .
Roger	Hear that? *We're* not being honest! What about your cat?
Joe	I had a cat . . .
Roger	And a dream?
Joe	And a dream and a father . . .
Roger	Who worked as a porter . . . and what else? A black tooth-brush?
Joe,	Yes, there's a black toothbrush . . . in my pocket . . .
Roger	What else?
Joe	There's a van that I drive . . . .
Roger	A van yes — come on — what else?
Joe	A sister who died . . .
Roger	Yes, what else?
Joe	A bomb in my bag . . .
Roger	Yes, what else . . .
Joe	A dream I had when I . . . .
Roger·	Dream. Yes. Come on, come on, come on . . . .
Peter	For God's sake, calm down.
Roger	Calm down? You had difficulty calming down when he said that your wife was over-sexed . . . .
Maureen	*(Laughing)* Ha. Who said that?
Peter	Don't you dare speak about my wife like that.
Suzy	Hold it, hold it, folks.
Roger	Well, it's true.
Peter	It's not bloody-well true.
Suzy	*(Shouting)* I said hold it right there! *(Silence. Rita sobs)*
Suzy	Okay now, quietly. I just want to know one thing. What did you just say, Joe?
Joe	Me?
Suzy	Yes you. About your bag.
Joe	My bag?
Suzy	Come on, Joe. Did you mean what you said?

Peter	What did he say?
Roger	Rubbish — he's been talking rubbish for so long . . .
Suzy	Quiet Roger. Joe, did you not say that there was a bomb in your bag?
Joe	Oh that. Yes.
Rita	A bomb?
Suzy	Shhh, Rita. Is it true, Joe?
Roger	How can you expect an honest answer to that?
Suzy	Joe, I'm asking you — is it true?
Joe	Yes, it's in my bag.
Peter	A bomb! What bag? Where's his bag?
Maureen	Quiet, Peter.
Peter	Don't quiet me.
Suzy	Is it in your bag outside the door, Joe?
Joe	Yes.
Peter	For Christ's sake — is he serious?
Roger	Is he stammering — that's the question. He only stammers when he's serious. Will you never learn.
Joe	*(Stammering)* It's outside the do . . do . . door.
Roger	There now — he's done it for us. All panic now.
Peter	Oh my God — my merciful God! Maureen?
Maureen	Stop that, Peter — be quiet.
Suzy	*(Calmly)* And this bomb, Joe — when will it explode?
Joe	I don't know. I just set the timer. I don't know.
Peter	Jesus Christ, Maureen — he set the timer . . . the bomb . . . .
Maureen	Stop it, Peter!
Peter	Stop it? You stop it — stop stopping me!
Maureen	Suzy, what can we do now?
Roger	Oh for Heaven's sake, he has you all going again. He'll apologise in a minute.
Suzy	No Roger, this is no joke anymore. I'm going to phone Paddy and have the police called . . . check this out . . . we got to do this thing . . .
Roger	Well, do that by all means, if you wish, but . . . .
Joe	Phone's not working.
Peter	What? What do you mean? Are we . . . all locked in here with a bloody bomb . . .
Suzy	The phone's okay, Peter — just relax. *(Takes the key from her shirt, goes to the phone)*
Roger	Just relax, everyone — nothing to worry about Rita — just prepare to laugh at Joe's latest joke.

Rita	*(Rising)* I'd like to go home now . . . .
Roger	It's only a game, Rita. Lie back there. Rest.
Rita	You were shouting, Roger.
Peter	If it's true about this bomb, I'll kill that bastard . . . .
Maureen	*(Stiffly)* If it's true, darling, you won't need to.
Peter	What the hell are you talking about?
Roger	She's right, Peter. And if it isn't true — which it's not — I'll help you to kill him anyway.
Suzy	*(Tapping phone)* Hello, hello, Jeez, that's strange. Hello . . .
Peter	What's wrong? Is it not working?
Suzy	No, it's okay. Just getting a line here. Hello . . . .
Peter	*(Jumping up)* Here, let me try.
Maureen	*(Laughing)* Ah good — Peter will fix it.
Suzy	It's okay, Peter . . .
Peter	*(Taking phone)* Jesus Christ — it's dead.
Roger	Dead? What do you mean?
Rita	*(Getting up)* Let me try — I have a phone that sometimes . . .
Roger	Rita, sit down — I'll see to it. You must rest.
Peter	Not a bloody sound.
Roger	Sit down Rita. It'll come back.
Peter	*(Finding torn flex)* Jesus, Look! Look! The phone wrecked. He's wrecked the phone.
Maureen	*(Rising)* Now Peter, come here. We'll ask Joe.
Suzy	*(Shouting to Joe)* Did you do this? Did you? Answer me — did you?
Roger	What? Did he break . . . .?
Peter	*(Laughing wildly)* Jesus, he's going to kill us all — he really is. We're all dead . . . .
Suzy	Did you? Answer! Did you?
Joe	Yesssss. *(Jumps up and runs towards the Contemplation Room. Is held by Roger)*
Roger	Just a moment *(Joe falls to the ground)*
Peter	*(Rushes over and kicks Joe)* Bastard! Killer!
Maureen	Stop that . . . Peter! Stop that!
Rita	*(Banging on entrance door)* Help! Help! Oh, Tom, Tom, Tom . . . .
Peter	*(Catching Joe by throat)* You bastard — I'm going to make sure you're the first to go . . .
Roger	Is there a bomb? Let him talk. Is there?
Maureen	*(Pulling at Peter)* No Peter, no. Let him be . . .
Roger	Is there a bomb?

Peter	I'll choke the truth out of him.
Suzy	Hold it! Hold it, I said.
Maureen	He can't breathe, he can't breathe. Let him go.
Roger	Let him tell us — is there a bomb?
	(Catches Joe by hair. Peter is pulled back by Maureen)
Joe	You're all supposed to be controlled — but you're frightened — just like her, just like her.
Peter	*(Kicks at Joe)* Is there a bomb?
Maureen	Coward! Let him be, coward!
Peter	Don't call me that, you.
Rita	Tom, Tom, Tom, Tom.
Peter	Will you stop that shouting.
Suzy	Yeah, shut-up Rita — the place is soundproof . . .
Peter	*(Kicks at Joe again)* Bastard!
Joe	My sister was frightened like you all . . . she was frightened, every night, after you'd finished with her . . .
Roger	Don't start that again — is there a bomb?
Suzy	Hold it! Come on, Joe — tell us about your sister.
Roger	Fairy tale time again. What about the bomb? What about the phone?
Suzy	If you two don't stop, we'll get nothing out of him. What happened to her, Joe?
Joe	All your in-depth analysis, your here-and-now debates — you did that to her. You all remind me of her now — frightened. All your prying . . .
Peter	Jesus, what's he talking about?
Suzy	Go on, Joe.
Joe	And then you left her, went back to your comfortable bungalows, purged of all your imaginary hang-ups, back to your ex-Group conventions, your cocktail parties . . . but *she* was quiet when she got home . . .
Rita	I can't hear him. What did he say?
Roger	He's talking rubbish again.
Suzy	Easy. Yes Joe?
Joe	She was like all of you — frightened, mad, waiting, silent . . . . after you all had left her . . .
Maureen	I didn't know your sister, Joe?
Roger	There's no sister . . .
Suzy	Shut-up, all of you. Joe, listen carefully. Nobody knew your sister, not anyone here . . . we never did anything . . . .
Roger	The little bastard hasn't got a sister at all . . .

Joe	Yes, you're right — but I had one — until she climbed down the railway embankment, waited for the train to come and threw herself under the wheels . . . she escaped, smeared along the tracks for a hundred yards . . . .
Maureen	No, Joe, No . . .
Suzy	We never knew her . . .
Joe	Just different faces in a different time . . . but it was all of you . . . her body along the railway line . . .
Roger	Wait a minute! That's the story of his cat . . . his dream . . . not his sister . . . .
Peter	He's mad . . . he's mad . . .
Roger	It's his cat he's talking about . . . his dream . . .
Joe	See if it's a dream — when the bomb explodes!
Roger	*(Gripping him by the hair again)* Is there . . .?
Peter	*(Kicking out at Joe)* Blast you to hell . . . .
Maureen	*(Pulling at Peter)* Peter, for God's sake, let him go . . .
Peter	Shut-up — get away from me . . .
Roger	Is there? Is there a bomb?
Maureen	Coward! Coward! Coward! *(As Peter grabs Joe)*
Peter	Coward am I? I suppose Marcus Dalton was a better man.
Rita	*(Banging on door)* Help me, Tom, Help me.
Maureen	Yes, Marcus Dalton was a better man. At least he was a man. He was a man.
Peter	Ah, it's all out now.
Maureen	Yes it is. He was a real man — not a coward!
Rita	Tom, Tom, Tom . . .
Suzy	Get away from that door, Rita — the bags are outside . . .
Rita	*(Runs to the Contemplation Room)* Help me . . . ! *(Peter and Roger kneel beside Joe, hitting him)*
Suzy	Stop it, for Christ's sake, stop it! Get to the Contemplation Room! Quick!
Peter & Roger	Liar! Bastard! Liar, tell us, tell us . . .
Maureen	Cowards, cowards — Half-men, you're only half-men! *(Joe goes limp, falls over. Silence as all watch)*
Maureen	Oh my God . . . my God . . . Oh, my God . . . my God . . .

LIGHTS OUT. END OF SCENE ONE. ACT TWO

SCENE TWO

Joe is lying on the floor. Stage is otherwise deserted. Hold for fifteen seconds. Contemplation Room door is unlocked and slowly opened. Maureen looks out.

Maureen	He doesn't seem to have moved at all. Do you think he's dead?
Peter	Will you close that bloody door. If the bomb goes off now, we'll all be blown to . . .
Maureen	Suzy, don't you think we ought to see if he's dead?
Suzy	*(Looking out)* Well, yeah, okay. Roger, would you like to see if he's . . . . alright?
Roger	Me? You don't seriously expect me to walk out into a damn explosion . . .
Suzy	Peter, will you go?
Peter	I'm bloody sure I won't
Maureen	Well, I didn't really expect a hero like you to go out anyway.
Peter	You go — you're so interested in him.
Maureen	I *will* go.
Peter	And close the bloody door after you.
Suzy	Okay, Okay, Maureen. I'll go.
Roger	*(Appearing)* No, stay, I'll look at him.
Maureen	Is he breathing? See if he's breathing.
Roger	I can't see from here *(Moves nearer)* Joe?
Peter	Will someone close that door.
Roger	No, no — don't close it!
Suzy	It's okay, Roger — we won't.
Roger	Joe? Can you hear me? Joe?
Joe	*(Not moving)* Roger, what's going to happen?
Roger	He's alive. He's just spoken.
Maureen	Thank God. What did he say?
Peter	He asked for you, I suppose.
Maureen	Shut-up. What did he say, Roger?
Roger	Joe, are you alright? *(Silence)* He just asked what is going to happen. That's all.
Peter	Jesus, that's great. He's the one who planted the bloody bomb.
Joe	*(Quietly)* No bomb . . . no bomb. All a game . . . all a game, Roger. For the Session. A here-and-now.
Suzy	What did he say, Roger?

63

Roger	He says there's no bomb *(To Joe)* Are you sure? How can we be sure?
Maureen	*(Laughs)* There's no bomb. It was all fun. Great.
Joe	No bomb . . . all games . . . just games . . you shouldn't have hit me . . . I'm dying . . . . I'm dying . . .
Suzy	What did he say, Roger?
Roger	Nothing . . . . he's alright *(To Joe)* Now come on, Joe — is there a bomb or not?
Joe	No bomb, Nothing . . . I want to go to the jacks, Roger. I'm sick . . .
Suzy	How's he, Roger?
Roger	There's no bomb — he thinks he's going to be sick.
Suzy	*(Coming across to Joe)* Is that right, Joe?
Joe	Yes, I'm going to be sick . . .
Suzy	No, about the bomb . . .
Joe	No bomb . . . all games . . . Session games . . . therapy . . . I'm sorry . . . I want to go to the jacks . . .
Roger	He means the loo. I think he's telling the truth.
Maureen	Joe? Are you alright?
Suzy	He's just been out for a few hours, that's all.
Roger	Try to stand . . . slowly.
Peter	Florence bleedin' Nightingale attends to the virile troops!
Maureen	*(To Peter)* I'll hold your virile little hand in a minute. *(To Joe)* How do you feel, Joe?
Rita	*(Appears)* What's happening?
Joe	I want to be sick . . . the jacks . . .
Suzy	Okay, let him . . . Roger, help him walk.
	(Roger and Joe cross to Contemplation Room)
Rita	Did it explode? Is he dead?
Peter	Yes, it exploded. We're all in bloody Hell — they're taking him up to Heaven!
Suzy	It's alright, Rita — there's no bomb — you just sit down.
Joe	*(Shaking off Roger)* It's alright. I can find it myself.
Roger	Are you sure, Joe? *(Joe enters the Contemplation Room)*
Suzy	Okay, okay folks — just relax now. Sit down, everyone. Sit down.
Roger	*(To Rita)* How do you feel?
Rita	I took a turn. Would you like a sweet?
Roger	Oh, no thanks.
Suzy	Not for me, Rita.
Rita	I'll keep them for later. *(Pause)* You were shouting, Roger.

	I remember.
Roger	Yes, I don't know . . . why. I mean . . . I was hitting him. I never, *never* did that to anyone.
Suzy	So why don't we explore that now? Let's not waste the Session. Let's use it to explore our true feeling about . . .
Peter	Marcus Dalton, for example.
Suzy	The Session can still work for each of us, Peter.
Joe	*(From room)* Hey, family.
	(The Contemplation Room door is noisely and ominously bolted by Joe. The group reacts to this)
Suzy	Joe? You okay, Joe?
Joe	Yes. In my bag, outside the door, there's a bomb.
Peter	What? Jesus Christ!
Suzy	*(Jumping up)* What did you say, Joe?
Joe	You're all sitting beside it — it's due to go off. In my bag . . .
	(All run to the Contemplation Room)
Rita	Open up, open up — open this door at once
Roger	Rita, don't scream . . . don't
Maureen	No don't, Rita.
Peter	*(Kicking door)* I'll kill you, I'll kill you . . .
Roger/	
Peter	Open the door, open the door . . . .
	(Entrance door is opened. Paddy stands looking. He is carrying some bags).
Paddy	Good morning *(Pauses, looking at the panic)*
	Good morning. *(Shouts)* I said Good Morning!
	(All turn. Silence)
Paddy	Here we are — the sun is up, the streets are aired, it's time for all of us to . . .
Suzy	*(Controlled)* Paddy, look Paddy now — is that Joe's bag you've got there?
Paddy	This one — yes.
Peter	Get to hell out of here with it!
Roger	There's a bomb . . .
Suzy	Take it easy, for God's sake . . .
Paddy	Bomb? What bomb?
Rita	I want to go now *(Moves towards door)*
Roger	*(Holds her)* Don't move, Rita.
Suzy	Now listen, Paddy — turn and chuck that bag down the stairs . . .
Paddy	Chuck it where?.

Maureen	Just throw it away, Paddy.
Peter	There's a bloody time-bomb in that bag!
Suzy	Chuck it away, Paddy . . . Now.
Paddy	There's nothing in this bag . . .
Roger	There is . . .
Maureen	Throw it away . . .
Paddy	There's not . . .
Peter	Are we going to stand here while he argues . . .
Suzy	There's a bomb in it — throw it away . . .
Paddy	There's nothing in it — I looked.
Suzy	You looked?
Paddy	I . . . eh . . . I supervised all the bags . . . *(Begins to open bag)*
Peter	No . . . Jesus . . . No . . . .
Suzy	Paddy . . . . don't . . .
Paddy	*(Empties bag onto floor)* See? Nothing. Towel, soap, a book, a clock, a spanner, a toilet roll, box of envelopes, bunch of keys . . . *(Silence)*
Suzy	You're not supposed to do that . . . to look into bags.
Paddy	Well, I sometimes just . . . eh . . . supervise the bags, as they say . . . *(Door of Contemplation Room opens. Joe appears)* . . . . Ah, hello, sunshine — hey, what happened to you?
Peter	*(Rushes over to hit Joe)* Bastard . . . Liar . . .
Paddy	Hey, what's going on?
Suzy	Okay, take it easy . . .
Roger	*(Holding Peter)* Leave him be, now. Peter, leave him.
Suzy	Now, Joe, what's all this about?
Joe	What?
Roger	*(Resigned)* He asks 'what'!
Suzy	You know what. Why did you do this? Why did you try to ruin my Session?
Joe	My bag! *(Sees contents on floor)* What happened to my bag?
Paddy	I . . . eh . . . they were looking for a bomb, sunshine.
Joe	A bomb?
Paddy	They said that there was a bomb . . . in your bag.
Suzy	That's enough, Paddy. Pick up these things.
Paddy	Yes, Miss Bernstein.
Joe	There's no bomb in my bag.
Paddy	I know sunshine, I told them that.
Suzy	That's enough, Paddy — do as I say
	(Paddy gathers Joe's belongings into the bag)

	Look people, we have a lot to talk about here . . . so let's relax for a while . . . .
Peter	Relax my arse — I've had enough of this — therapy . . .
Joe	*(Quietly)* Ha — that's good alright.
Suzy	Peter, look people — if we don't sort this out, then it's all wasted, all worthless, we'll have achieved nothing . . . I'll . . . we've . . . . . We'll have failed in our Session.
Peter	That's right, I'm going. Come on, Maureen.
Maureen	Don't talk to me like that.
Rita	I'd like to go home too.
Roger	Would you really?
Rita	Yes.
Roger	If you like I can drive you to . . .
Rita	If my husband were alive he'd drive me — he was a quiet, gentle person . . .
Roger	I understand.
Rita	He used to drive me everywhere. He was gentle . . .
Roger	I understand.
Suzy	Hold it, hold it — we can sort this out through communication — just relax . . . .
Joe	. . . relate, communicate *(To Paddy)* That's what we do here.
Paddy	Yeah — signs of it! *(Picks up bags)*
Roger	I. . . . I'll get your coat from Paddy.
Suzy	Look, will you all just sit down, for Christ's sake . . .
Paddy	*(To Roger)* Here you are Sir. *(Holds out hand for a tip)* It's been a pleasure attending to you . . .
Roger	Thank you — goodbye, Suzy. Are you ready, Rita?
Rita	Yes Roger. *(To Paddy)* Thank you, young man.
Paddy	It's been a pleasure bringing you your meals and sweeping up after you *(Waits for a tip)*
Rita	Yes, thank you. Have I my tablets? Yes. Goodbye to you all now. *(To herself)* I didn't like the shouting — I take turns, you know . . . *(Leaves with Roger)*
Peter	Now, are you coming or not?
Paddy	Ah, your bag, sir — it's been a pleasure attending . . .
Suzy	Will you knock it off, Paddy!
Paddy	I was just giving him his bag . . .
Suzy	Peter. We've had problems, but if we scatter, the Group will have failed — and I'm determined not to allow that to happen . . .

Peter	Are you coming?
Maureen	No!
Peter	Will I send Marcus Dalton over for you then?
Maureen	Don't bother.
Peter	*(Indicates Joe)* Him, is it? Mother of God, is it him?
Maureen	Wouldn't you like to know.
Peter	Well, *I'm* going . . . now . . .
Maureen	Well go! Now!
Peter	Blast you, Maureen — I'm not going to wait for long, mind you . . . . I'm not waiting for long . . .
Paddy	Goodbye sir, it's been a pleasure . . . *(Peter leaves)*
Suzy	Paddy — sweep! Sweep out the Contemplation Room and shut-up!
Paddy	Yes, Miss Bernstein. I'll leave your bag here, sunshine. *(Goes to Contemplation Room)*
Joe	Grand. Thanks Paddy.
Suzy	Okay, okay — go. The Group Session is closed — failed. You've all failed. *(Picks up clip)* You're all supposed to sign this, you know. What the hell. Forget it. *(Writes on clip).* *(Silence)*
Maureen	You're priceless Joe — do you know that? You're a dream-maker — a nightmare-maker. *(Laughs)*
Joe	Yes — that's life or something.
Maureen	No you really are. I don't know why you did those things.
Joe	Don't you?
Suzy	The Group is closed — we're locking up *(She exits to Contemplation Room)*
Maureen	Yes. Well, it was different . . . a bit different.
Joe	Was it?
Maureen	Oh it was. *(Pause)* Well, I must go now, Joe.
Joe	To Peter?
Maureen	Of course — why not? Why wouldn't I?
Joe	Yes. He builds good bungalows.
Maureen	Don't belittle it, Joe — he does. He works hard.
Joe	You have a good home . . .
Maureen	. . . house . . .
Joe	Split-level . . .
Maureen	It's something.
Joe	Split-level something . . . .
Maureen	Well, mustn't keep Peter waiting.
Joe	. . . or he'll be up again.

Maureen	Huh, there's a joke there somewhere.
Joe	Yes.
Maureen	So, goodbye Joe.
Joe	Goodbye.
Suzy *(off)*	Paddy, you better lock that door downstairs.
Maureen	Locks on doors, bricks on windows, Peter waiting . . . *(Leaves)*
	(Joe picks up his bag. Paddy comes from room)
Paddy	Ah, sunshine — still here?
Joe	Just going . . .
Paddy	*(Quietly)* Jaysus, I warned you, didn't I? Said you weren't the type, didn't I?
Joe	You did.
Paddy	What the hell did they do to you?
Joe	Oh nothing. Curiosity — nearly killed the cat. Remember, you said that.
Paddy	Don't remind me, sunshine. I'll tell you one thing though — if it's not being too personal. Your little stammer. It's gone, isn't it?
Joe	Oh yes. It is.
Paddy	Noticed that as soon as I came in. You're talking grand now.
Suzy	*(Emerging)* Paddy? Paddy, I thought I told you to lock the door and to . . .
Paddy	Yes, Miss Bernstein — I'm going. Good luck now, sunshine.
Joe	Goodbye Paddy. *(Paddy leaves)*
Suzy	Alright sir — you can go now. We're closed.
Joe	Yes. It went quite well, didn't it?
Suzy	Will you please get out.
Joe	A real in-depth analysis — true colours showing all around.
Suzy	Are you going?
Joe	Yes. *(Turns to leave)* Oh, about the honesty thing.
Suzy	Yes?
Joe	Texaleto.
Suzy	Texaleto? What the hell are you talking about? Don't play games with me.
Joe	Where you came from. You told Roger. Remember?
Suzy	Look, the place is closed, so will you please get out and close the door.
Joe	It's not in Utah.
Suzy	What isn't?
Joe	Texaleto. It's in Arizona. Texaleto Arizona. It's worth

69

knowing because I told Paddy. He knows now. Arizona.
(Joe leaves. Suzy waits. She rushes to the door)

Suzy   Hey, I'll tell you about that. *(Silence)* Hey, I said I'd tell you. *(Silence)* Hey, what about the phone you broke? What about that? *(Silence)* And the way you wrecked the Session. What about that? *(Returns from door. Pauses thoughtfully. Flings clip-board across the room)* God-damn freaks! Who could run a Therapy Session with them!!

BLACKOUT

THE PEACOCK THEATRE

In 1926 W. B. Yeats founded the original Peacock Theatre in two up-stairs room above the Pit Cafe of the old Abbey. The present Peacock was incorporated in the new Abbey building and officially opened in 1967. A small, well-equipped theatre under the main auditorium, it is an intimate and exciting theatrical space which can be adapted to semi-arena or proscenium arch presentation.

During the past twelve years, the theatre has been a showcase for new playwriting, reinterpretation of works from the classical repertoire, children's theatre, and plays in the Irish language. New writing has always played an implicit role in the theatre's programme and Thomas Kilroy, Thomas Murphy, Brendan Behan, Stewart Parker, Heno Magee, Desmond Hogan, Jennifer Johnston and Maeve Binchy are but a few of the numerous writers who have had their work premiered in the Peacock.

Apart from its theatrical activity, the Peacock also runs an active pro-gramme of lunchtime presentations, concerts, poetry readings, and exhibitions.